To
my Father and Mother

To
my Father and Mother

D. G. Tuler

THE TEACH YOURSELF BOOKS

THE CHRISTIAN FAITH

By
DAVID H. C. READ
M.A., B.D.
Chaplain to the University of Edinburgh

ENGLISH UNIVERSITIES PRESS LTD
LONDON

First printed 1955

Printed in Great Britain for the English Universities Press, Limited,
by Richard Clay and Company, Ltd., Bungay, Suffolk

INTRODUCTION

THIS book is written for those who want to know what the Christian Faith means as a system of thought and as a spur for action. I hope that it is expressed in terms that do not require any theological vocabulary or Church background. Its purpose is primarily to explain rather than to commend, although it is obvious that no one writing from within the Christian tradition can view it as a detached observer. Perhaps I might add that, if I were writing a book to commend the Faith for acceptance, it would be on the ground that it is *true*, and not just that it provides a useful basis for social action or psychological adjustment.

The book was not difficult to write when I kept in mind various friends and acquaintances who have sceptical but enquiring minds. It was much more difficult to write when I thought of the variety of Christian tradition. It is quite impossible to write of the Christian Faith in such a way as to do justice to every point of view. I write as a minister of the Church of Scotland, and cannot, even if I wanted to, disentangle myself from that Presbyterian background. But I hope that I have kept in mind the wider inheritance of the Church Catholic and that the book will be acceptable as an expression of the essential content of that which Christians hold in common.

I have not quoted much from other writers (except the Biblical), although I am indebted to more than I can number or name. It has seemed to me better to refer the reader to specific books at the end of each chapter. These are only examples out of a wide range of theological literature to which I hope this book may prove some kind of introduction.

There is a slick catch-word beloved of preachers which says that " Christianity is not taught but caught ". That serves to remind us of the limitations of such an attempt as this. " Teach yourself Christianity " would hardly be a possible title for a book, although it would make an admirable motto for a life. It is, however, possible to learn what the Christian Faith is about, and this is the purpose of the following pages.

DAVID H. C. READ.

CONTENTS

CHAPTER I

THE BASIS OF BELIEF

"YOU have faith," says the sceptic, "so you are entitled to indulge in the luxury of religious beliefs. I haven't; and that's the end of the matter."

Discussion of religious topics today is apt to founder at this point. Whether it is the Christian Faith that is under consideration or some other, the underlying assumption is normally that some people are so constituted as to be able to believe while others are not. Religious people are those who have succeeded in adding to the normal equipment of everyday beliefs, supplied by experience, common sense, and scientific discovery, a set of comforting convictions about an unseen world, which lies totally beyond the sphere of the obvious and reasonable. These they hold with tenacity but are incapable apparently of communicating intelligibly to others. On this view the Christian Faith is a live option in the department of religion, but the department itself is only open to those who have inherited or acquired this sixth sense that enables them to believe in the reality of this invisible world. Both sceptics and Christians are inclined to speak and behave as though there were this great gulf fixed between those who have " faith " and those who have not.

Religious debate thus tends to be both more tolerant and more abortive than in previous ages. It is more tolerant because on the whole the modern believer is sympathetic towards those who cannot

believe and much less likely than Christians in the
past to associate atheism with moral delinquency—
an attitude revealed by the derivation of the word
" miscreant "; literally, " one who believes amiss ".
And the modern sceptic, unlike the militant atheist
of former generations, is usually open to conviction.
He is slow to dismiss as entirely illusory the evidences
of religion simply because they lie outside the range
of his present experience. Yet this tolerance on
each side is apt to lead to the situation where a dead-
lock is reached. Discussion becomes abortive because it is being assumed that faith is a kind of
psychological quirk that provides an entry into a
region of comforting, possibly interesting, but ultimately unnecessary convictions.

Before we can profitably consider the content of
the Christian Faith we must challenge this way of
thinking about religion. We might notice to start
with that it is quite foreign to the New Testament.
Christianity has never been the faith of a religious
élite, the possessors of a mysterious mystic faculty of
belief. From the beginning it has been professed
by an extraordinary variety of men and women, by
no means all of whom have been what we would call
" religious types ". It is remarkable that its greatest
opponents, for instance, have not usually been the
sceptics but the " religious "—the upholders of
another faith, that of the Pharisees in the first
century or that of the Communists in the twentieth.
Its adherents have been as varied a cross-section of
humanity as those who crowd the pages of the
Gospels. Again, Christianity is not set forth in the
Bible or the Church as a set of interesting speculations about an invisible world, but as an affirmation
about the life that we have to live here and now.

The Gospel proclaims that life can be transformed in response to the action of the living God, but the extent and number of our beliefs about the invisible may have little relevance to our faith. Christ himself never speaks of faith as if it were a mysterious capacity for believing things that the normal man finds incredible. "Have faith in God "[1] he says, as if this were a possibility for all; and clearly not all of us can accept in an instant even the simplest of the Christian creeds. A reading of the Gospels will lead to the discovery that what he means by faith is an attitude of life that is open to all men. "Why are ye so fearful?"[2] he once asked the disciples, "how is it that ye have no faith?" He does not say: "Why are ye intellectual doubters? how is it that ye have no faith?" For him apparently the opposite of faith was not so much doubt as *fear*.

This book will be concerned with doctrines, or— if you like—dogma. Christianity has no more need to apologize for its intellectual formulations than any other activity of the human spirit, and the time is happily passing when Christians boasted of not caring about creeds. Yet it must be stated as plainly as possible that these doctrines and creeds are not the heart of the Faith. They are reflections upon an encounter with God. The reflections are not arbitrary, but have, as we shall see, weighty authority for the Christian; yet it is the encounter that is primary. The Christian Faith is rooted in something that God has done; and Christian belief issues in a way of life. We are not dealing with " mere beliefs ". A living religion is never concerned with adding little bits of unfounded belief to

[1] Mark xi. 22.   [2] Mark iv. 40.

our normal mental equipment. To put it in another way, real religion is not a kind of attic in our human habitation where we store superfluous furniture and pay occasional visits. Rather is it the foundation on which all the rest ultimately depends. "Attic-religion" exists; but it is really superstition—which is literally that which "stands above" what we are really entitled to believe. All religions may contain an element of superstition (and Christianity in practice has not been an exception), but essentially they are attempts to answer questions that are not superfluous but essential. Superstitions are a set of irrational beliefs that we tack on to the data of common sense, and they are usually concerned with minor incidents of life, such as walking under ladders or wearing certain clothes at weddings. Religious faiths deal with the fundamental decisions by which our life is ruled. Their formulation may be *supra-rational*, since all our basic beliefs in life are beyond the sphere of rational proof; but they need not be *irrational*, in the sense of clearly contradicting the evidence of our minds and senses.

We must elaborate a little this conception of religious faith as a basic attitude to life, for it is essential to any true understanding of what the Christian Faith is about. No approach to the message of Christianity can be fruitful which regards it simply as a set of esoteric propositions to be swallowed by a super-human effort of credulity. Yet this is the assumption of a great many of our contemporaries.

We might begin by asking what has caused so many to regard religion as a rather problematical "extra" to the ordinary business of life, and faith as a mysterious faculty for accepting it. I believe

it has to do with the way in which most of us have
been taught to view the world we live in. A certain
kind of picture has been built up in us from our
earliest days, and this picture, which we may never
have consciously examined, has determined our outlook on such matters as religious beliefs. According to this picture " I " (the perceiving subject,
taken for granted) am faced with a world containing a vast number of objects ranging from atoms
to stars. These objects are real. We know they
are there. We can observe them; touch them;
measure them: or, if we cannot, we know that the
scientist has an instrument for doing so. Ultimately, according to what we have been told, all
these apparently solid objects consist of atoms in
motion (with a good deal more motion than atom),
but we are still left with a world that can be directly
known. This is the real world, lying outside us
—measurable, predictable. Even if the modern
scientist makes it sound infinitely mysterious, we
feel that it has a certain solid reality. The formulæ
of the laboratory may be as remote to us as New
Testament Greek, but we can all see the results of
them—television sets, bombs, cars, and washing-
machines. According to this picture, then, this
objective, manipulable world is what we have to
reckon with. And everything that conveys information about it is real knowledge. Now when the
religious man comes along with his talk of God,
prayer, sin, heaven, and the like, we just cannot fit
them into this picture. They are not measurable
things. Neither telescope nor microscope show any
trace of an object, or even a movement, that could
be called God or the soul. Therefore we feel that
these things, whatever they are, cannot be *real* in the

same way as the moon, a fountain-pen, or a polio germ. If they exist at all, then they belong to a sphere outside the picture, and we have got to accept them on somebody's word. To believe in them firmly is thus the privilege, or the illusion, of a select few.

If this is roughly a true account of the kind of picture with which we tend to operate today, then it is not surprising that there is a good deal of latent scepticism as to the truth of the Christian Faith, or any other system of religious belief. What is surprising is that the picture itself should have survived. For it belongs to a past era in the story of scientific and philosophic thought. That we are still affected by it is an example of the time-lag that always intervenes between the thinking of the pioneers and its popular assimilation. This explains the curious fact that the leading scientists of today are much less inclined to claim universal validity for the scientific approach than the sixth-form science student. The fact is that this way of considering our relation to the world, and estimating what is true or real, is at variance not only with what the scientists and philosophers have been telling us for years, but also with the dictates of enlightened common sense.

The philosophers, of course, have always challenged any easy assumption that we know what is real. They question our right to assume that what our senses tell us conveys any true information about the outside world. When I say, " I know that this table exists ", they begin by asking what I mean by " knowing ", by " existence ", and who " I " am. If this sounds to the layman like clever-clever talk designed to confuse a simple question, we might stop to think whether the matter is indeed as simple as we have assumed. By what right can we assume the reality of an outside world of solid objects? Do we really *know* that the sun exists " out there " independently of all who see it? Is it not rather true that I am aware of myself, the " I " that is observing the sun, much more certainly and surely than of the sun itself. But there is no instrument to reveal this " I " to me: it cannot be proved to exist along the usual lines. My body and my brain can be observed in action, but there is no way of catching and examining the self that does the observing. Again, am I sure that I *know* that water is composed of hydrogen and oxygen with greater certainty than I know that I ought to do good rather than evil? Yet no one can measure good and evil with an instrument. It is clear that here we are on infinitely debatable ground, and I am not trying to advocate any particular philosophy of knowing. What we can surely assert is that the notion that truth consists in what we can discover of an outside world through the appropriate instruments can hardly withstand serious thought.

But what has shattered the familiar picture of a real world of solid things standing over against me and containing all that we really know, more than any query of philosophy or common sense, is the further investigation of science itself into the nature of the world we live in. It is not simply that scientists have tended to acknowledge with increasing frequency in recent years the restricted nature of their researches, leaving open many other avenues of approach to the real, but that the physicists are now reckoning with a picture of the world far removed from that of a complicated movement of atoms in surrounding space, a world of objective fact, detached from the human observer. As far as the scientifically uneducated, like the writer, can understand it, the modern physicist has given up the notion of " space " as a simple surrounding element in which things happen in the outside world, and has now come to include the observer, the " I ", as an all-important factor in the understanding of our world. Einstein, Planck, and the modern nuclear physicists have destroyed the old picture of matter as something solid existing in space independent of the observer, and are now operating with a picture of the universe which is beyond the capacity of most of us to understand, but which at least draws attention again to the fundamental importance of the observing subject, the " I ".

Those whose job it is to attempt to commend the Christian Faith have to be careful in the use they make of modern scientific discoveries. As much nonsense can be talked about science proving religion as of disproving it. It would be quite wrong to give the impression that modern science is in some way demonstrating the validity of the religious hypothesis. Religion has never been dependent on the discoveries of science, although some of its pronouncements have been profoundly modified by them. The fundamental assertions of faith can be neither proved nor disproved by an examination of the nature of the physical world. What does seem to have happened by the recent advance of the physical and other sciences is an undermining of the basis of materialism in its cruder forms. The dividing-line between matter and spirit is now as indeterminate in science as it has always been in the Christian Faith, although the scientist might not express himself in just this way. Certainly to believe that the only reality ultimately consists of infinitesimal particles of matter moving according to rigidly determined laws now implies an act of credulity as great as has ever been demanded by any religion or superstition.

The relevance of the Christian Faith appears when we are finished with the false picture of our relationship to the " real " world of matter, and think again of how we find truth in the daily life of this " I ", confronted with all kinds of mysterious questions that demand an answer. Each successive generation begins to ask almost as soon as they have learned to speak: " Who am I ? " " What am I doing here? " " What is this world for? " " Where am I going? " These are the questions with which religion deals. They are real questions. The kind of truth involved is a more fundamental one than that of knowing the constituents of the atom. We have all to answer the question: " What shall I do? " The scientist himself has to decide whether or not it is worth his while to continue his researches. He is also a man who marries, votes in an election, perhaps plays in an orchestra or paints pictures. All these activities are of supreme importance in human life, and they are determined by the answers that we give to some of these fundamental questions. Faith is better defined as the motive power of a life based on answers to these questions than as any mere instrument of credulity.

It is, of course, often said today that these fundamental questions are meaningless; that they cannot possibly be answered. No one, it is claimed, can possibly know why the world came into existence, or what life is really meant to be. We should dismiss such questions from our minds and get on with the business of living. But what *is* the business of living? I may easily get up in the morning and have my breakfast without giving a passing thought to the meaning of existence (it is a parsonic fallacy that people are always asking themselves these deep questions); yet the pattern I am following is ultimately based on some kind of faith as to the meaning of life, what is worth doing. And every really serious decision that comes my way in practical matters demands from me an answer that I can only give on the assumption that life *has* some meaning. True or false; right or wrong—we make these judgments every day of our lives; and they imply that some standards exist—in other words, that we have made some act of faith as to what is worth doing, or worth believing, or worth becoming. That is what is meant when it is said that " we live by faith ".

Christian faith is an attitude to the mystery of life that determines our character and actions. It is this before it can be expressed in a series of propositions to be believed. To put it simply: when the first disciples decided to follow Jesus Christ they were saying, " This is the life I was meant to live; this is the human family to which I belong; and the world I live in is in the hands of the God and Father of Jesus Christ." They were adopting an attitude to life based on their encounter with Jesus Christ, and it affected every detail of their lives. It was only later that they came to reflect on their experience and set down in words what they now believed to be true about Christ, about men, and about our world. Whether we like it or not, the daily business of life compels each one of us to make decisions, and these decisions will be based, consciously or unconsciously, on our faith as to the meaning of life. Whatever we decide—to adopt the Christian Faith, or the Moslem, or the Communist, or any other system, even an agnostic one—we live by a faith we cannot prove. Even an atheist must act on a faith that there is no God, for he likewise cannot prove the validity of his assumption.

In the present confusion of belief there is a natural tendency for men and women to despair. Amid all the rival points of view, none of which can be proved mathematically or demonstrated scientifically, how can we possibly make a convincing choice? Yet life demands of us a choice. We must do this—or that; become this kind of person—or the other. To evade the choice is still a choice : it is to choose to live like an animal or vegetable. It is not surprising that in this situation there is a tendency to follow those who talk in the loudest voice, and to be attracted by totalitarian claims. Yet none of these claims or voices can resolve our personal problem. For we have to make a choice about *them*. Even to adhere to a faith that professes to have absolute truths is still the decision of our fallible minds. How shall we be guided?

The Christian Faith is one that accepts and respects this situation of mankind. It comes to us with a sure and certain sound, but never as an irresistible force that smashes the citadel of our wills. There is no way of presenting Christianity so that any intelligent person will be intellectually bound to accept it; yet, once it is accepted in faith it is found to be more intellectually satisfying than any rival view of the universe. There is, however, no way for anyone to avoid the decision of faith. Within Christianity this is sometimes a matter of absorbing it in childhood and never finding much difficulty with its doctrines throughout life. Others have much greater difficulty, and would describe their faith as being like following the light that has appeared to them, and hoping that the penumbra of darkness will become less. Others accept vaguely what has been taught to them, while deviating continually in the direction of other faiths. Others again find conviction of the truth of the Christian Faith sweeping in on them and banishing their previous doubts. Whatever our experience may be, some kind of personal acceptance is always involved. The decision has to be made; and we shall find that it is made as a response to that which has been revealed to us. We make our decision in this matter as we are confronted by what we know to be true. The Christian does not pump up faith out of the the recesses of his own soul. It is his Yes to the truth that comes to him with Jesus Christ.

It is reasonable to ask why we should commit our lives to the Christian answers to the " life-questions ". On what basis does the Christian make his decision? It is clear that the Christian Faith does come to us with certain credentials. Faith may be a leap, but it is not a leap in the dark. We would maintain, on the contrary, that it is a leap into the light—that the act of faith itself illuminates in turn many aspects of life and brings sense into what had been confusion. We are not, after all, left floundering so that it hardly matters which particular way of life we adopt. When I select a man for a job I may have a number of possible candidates, but I do not choose with a list and a pin. I use judgment, consider records and let them make their own impression on me. There is no way of reaching mathematical certainty that my choice is the right one. But, having examined the credentials, I must make the choice.

What could we call the credentials of Christianity?

(1) There is the Christian Church. It may seem surprising to begin with an organization which it is fashionable to distinguish from " true Christianity ". " I want to hear about the Christian Faith," you may be saying, " not about the Christian Church. I know this organized religion, with its entrenched dogmas and vested interest in orthodoxy. It is the Church that puts me off Christianity: how, then, can it be considered any kind of a credential? "

There is certainly a sense in which the nature and record of the Church as we know it tells against the truth of Christianity. " The one really formidable argument against the truth of the Christian religion ", it has been said, " is the record of the Christian Church." This, however, is to dwell on its failures and on the seamier side of Church history. There is another story. But quite apart from these judgments, we have to face the fact that from the beginning Christianity has been a Church. The Church is no after-thought, representing the fossilization of a living religion. Every single Christian doctrine or idea has come to us from the Church, and the Christian Faith is inseparable from it. I am speaking now of the Church in the sense of the community of Christians that has existed from the time of the apostles, and still exists in nearly every country in the world; and not of any particular denomination, nor primarily in the institutional sense of the word.

The Church exists. This is a fact—for a generation that is supposed to respect facts. Whatever we believe about its origins, or the truth of its dogmas, however confused we may be by the apparently rival sections into which it is broken, we cannot surely help being impressed by the unbroken existence of a community which, in a vast variety of languages, liturgies, and organizational forms, witnesses across the centuries and the frontiers to a Gospel of Jesus Christ. There is nothing comparable to this in the history of human institutions. It is as striking as the continued existence of the Jewish race (the two phenomena are not unconnected, as we shall see later). In particular, we Europeans stand in a very intimate relationship to this tradition, for the Church and its teachings have entered into the fabric of our communal life and have deeply influenced the basic assumptions of every one of us. There is really no such thing as an isolated Christian, the Christian without the Church. We may disclaim all membership, yet it is impossible for us to disentangle our beliefs in God or man from the living tradition of the Church. We have absorbed it from our parents, our schools, our literature, our entire history.

It will therefore be impossible to set forth the Christian Faith without thereby expounding the teaching of the Church. There is no other way of proceeding, however tempting it might be to try to spin a new version of the Faith out of the Bible and some pet private theories. (This is, in fact, continually being done, and new cults arise which, however much they differ from one another, have this in common: they believe themselves to be in possession of a key to the truth about Christianity that has been hidden from nineteen centuries of Church life and devotion.) Anyone who claims to be talking about the Christian Faith must surely be continually reckoning with the witness of the

Christian community throughout the world and across the centuries. And anyone who is looking for the credentials of Christianity must be impressed by its persistence, ubiquity, and vigour.

When we consider the Christian claims, then, we find ourselves confronted by this persistent and living tradition. Its strength and pedigree are not in themselves enough to guarantee for us the truth of the Christian Faith, but they are a weighty element to be pondered. We must guard against the temptation of a rootless age to consider traditions of any kind as *ipso facto* suspect. The existence of the Church means not only that these doctrines have a long history, but that they have sustained the life of the most remarkable supra-national community known to history, and are part of its living worship today. We do not therefore hold them as private speculations, but as the common beliefs by which this vast Christian family lives.

It is true that the Christian Church does not appear before us as a united family today. When we consider the multitude of its denominations, and the huge variety of its liturgies and confessions, it might seem that there is no such consensus to appeal to—no witness of *the* Christian Church to its Gospel. Yet, however much we deplore these divisions, we must not exaggerate their effect. The central truths of the Christian Faith which have been enshrined in the historic creeds are held in common by the overwhelming majority of Christian bodies. The World Council of Churches, representing some 180,000,000 non-Roman Catholic Christians, comes together on the basis of a confession of Jesus Christ as " God and Saviour "—and it is quite certain that on this point it is not divided from the belief of Roman

Catholics. Here, then, is an expression of faith of the most decisive and radical kind (as we shall see when we turn to examine its implications), one that is quite incompatible with rival views of the universe, and this is held in common by millions of men and women of every conceivable range of race, colour, education, cultural tradition, and language—and has been for twenty centuries. The convergence of belief is impressive. Even more impressive is the witness of worship, by which in a great variety of forms devotion is given to Christ as Lord. It is this Faith that we are to examine; and we must begin where we all first hear of it—in the community of the Church.

There is all the difference in the world between saying, "You must accept the Christian Faith because the Church knows the truth", and, "If you want to understand the Christian Faith you must reckon with the Church". Too often, in rebellion against what seems an intolerant claim on the part of the Church, sincere people have dismissed altogether this powerful credential of the Faith.

(2) Then there is the Bible. Everybody knows that Christians of all traditions claim to derive their doctrines from the Bible, and anyone who wants to examine the credentials of Christianity must clearly take into account these written records that have been so carefully preserved. But it is important to see just why and how the Bible books are to be taken into consideration.

The Bible has suffered a good deal from its friends. We are always being told what a good book it is. It is commended for everything from its moral content to its prose style. We are continually confronted with isolated verses of it used as ammunition in religious discussion. It is annotated, dissected, expounded; but we are seldom told just what place it holds as evidence for the Christian interpretation of life, as one of the credentials of the Faith. It is this point that concerns us here; not the devotional, historical, or liturgical use of the Bible in the Church or in the lives of individual Christians.

Although this book has not yet attempted to set down the essence of the Christian Faith, it is surely already apparent that it is concerned with a belief in a God whose nature and purposes are specially disclosed to us in the person and actions of Jesus Christ. This is the one whom the Churches serve and worship as Lord and God. Now this Christ appeared on earth as an historical person at a precise point in history. He was a member of the Jewish race and lived in the early days of the Roman Empire. If we want information about him we must look for documents as nearly contemporary as possible. What the books of the New Testament offer is first-hand evidence of the impression made by Jesus Christ on those who first responded to him and to his message. Since tremendous significance is attached in Christianity to the person of Christ and to the events surrounding his life, a unique authority attaches within the Church to the documents that contain this contemporary witness. Even to the non-believer the New Testament must for the same reasons be a book to reckon with in any attempt to understand what the Christian Faith is about. It is not simply, as is often supposed, that they can read in it the teaching of Jesus himself: they can find there clear evidence of the impact he made on his followers and on the world. It is because Christianity is an historical religion, because the Faith is closely tied

up with things that happened " under Pontius
Pilate " (as the Apostles' Creed puts it) that the New
Testament books have this unique importance. No
subsequent literature can have this evidential value:
they are derivative. There is no way of going
beyond or behind what the apostles have said in the
New Testament. For our Christian facts it is this
evidence—or none at all. And, without going into
any detail of literary or historical or textual criticism,
it is possible now to say that as a result of the most
intense labour of research we may have the greatest
confidence in the authenticity and integrity of the
records. No miraculous claim is made by most
Christians for the reporting of these events, but it
has stood up amazingly to the most rigorous critical
examination.

So far I have spoken only of the New Testament.
But the Bible as a whole displays an extraordinary
unity over its vast panorama of literary and religious
form. The New Testament is hardly understandable to us, except in the light of the Old. Jesus
came from the race whose strange and unique
history is recorded in its books; he himself was
steeped in them, and his followers interpreted his
life-work in terms of what they had to say. There
is scarcely a leading note of the New Testament that
cannot be traced back to the Old. They stand
together as witnesses to a slice of history (in the view
of the secular historian a small, and in many respects
an insignificant, slice) which has been determinative
for the moulding of much of human history on any
reading of that story, and which is of eternal significance for the human race according to Christian
belief. To understand the Christian Faith one must
listen to the voice of prophet and apostle.

We can see now why the Bible plays a vital rôle as a credential of the Faith, and why any exposition of the Faith must be in harmony with its witness. We considered the Church first of all because the living tradition is our first contact with Christianity and the most immediate evidence. But we know how easily tradition can be corrupted. An institution or organization can soon drift far from the desire and intention of the founder. Therefore the Church has always guarded the Scriptures as the norm or test of Christian truth. And from time to time the voice of Scripture has been heard anew challenging the assumptions or practices of the contemporary Church. Protestants believe that something like this happened at the time of the Reformation. The Reformers had no desire to found a new Church. The very idea would have horrified them. They wished to re-form the Church according to the Bible. Again, in our own time the Bible has become a power in the thinking of the Church at a time when modern Protestantism seemed likely to drift away from the central Christian tradition in the direction of a liberal humanism. The Word of God, the expression used to describe this witness of prophet and apostle to the revelation they recorded, is held in most parts of the Christian Church to be the " supreme rule of faith and life ".

When, therefore, this book sets out the content of the Christian Faith, it will always be, so far as the author is able, in harmony with Holy Scripture. This will not be by way of strings of supporting texts, or a mere reiteration of " The Bible says . . ."; for Christian doctrine cannot be read off the pages of the Bible as if it were a kind of theological Bradshaw. The authority of the Bible is not magical.

It lies in the intimate relation of these books to the event of Christ—meaning by that the entire circumstances surrounding his coming to this world. And as there is no other authority for this event except that which derives from the witness of the Bible, then all Christian doctrine must rest upon its testimony.

Here let me say that the sceptic and the seeker would be well advised to consider the evidence of the Bible with as open and fresh a mind as possible. It is particularly important that we should not come to these books with any pre-conceived ideas as to what they have to say, or what weight is to be given to each passage. In particular, we must beware of those who offer " keys " to the Scriptures. They need no keys. They are open for all to read. And theories of inspiration only bedevil the work of hearing what the writers are really saying. We need help of a practical and non-tendentious kind, such as is provided by commentaries and modern translations. But we do not need allegorical systems designed to wrest texts from their contexts to make them prove something about the times we live in. The churches have all got their " doctrines of Holy Scripture ", their understanding of what is meant by the Word of God. But for the enquirer no preliminary act of faith is demanded by the Biblical books. They make their own appeal. All we can say is: " Here are the written credentials of our faith; they come from a period of history we believe to be of supreme importance for mankind; in them you will find the witness to Jesus Christ; let them speak for themselves."

(3) It is clear, however, that the credentials of Christianity for any believer are not entirely to be described in terms of Church and Bible. No one

ever accepted the Chistian Faith simply because the Church taught it or the Bible recorded it. When we find a Christian giving as the grounds for his belief simply: " The Church says so " or " The Bible says so " we may well suspect a second-hand religion, a doctrinaire belief. We read that when Pilate asked Jesus: "Art thou the King of the Jews?" he answered with the words: " Sayest thou this thing of thyself, or did others tell it thee of me? "[1] Genuine religious faith always implies the ability to " say it of thyself". In other words, for the Christian the really vital credential is the inner conviction in his heart that these things are so.

It is here that we come across the real difficulty of communication. It is comparatively easy to show what the Church believes and whom she worships, and to summarize the message of the Bible—at least easy in comparison with showing a non-believer how this faith comes alive in one's own heart and mind. It might even look as if we had now come full circle and had returned to the abortive discussion between the man who has " faith " and the man who has not. I hope enough has been said to show that this is not the situation. For this inner conviction can come to any kind of human being whatever in response to the revelation of God—normally in the context of Church and Bible. How does it come about that what I have heard since infancy in the Church suddenly comes to have real meaning and infinite practical importance for *me*? What happens to make odd passages written centuries ago by prophet or apostle luminous and determinative for me *now*? The Christian answer to this question (to which we shall have to return at a later point) is that the

[1] St. John xviii. 33–34.

supreme credential of Christianity is the direct witness
of the Holy Spirit. By Holy Spirit we mean the
living God in action here and now. It is God himself who speaks to us through Bible and Church,
making their testimony alive for us. This way of
speaking may be comparatively meaningless to
those who have not yet attained any kind of Christian
conviction. But they will realize that there is an
inner logic in this conviction. The Christian Faith
is about God—a God who is the sole ultimate
authority and controller of all things. He cannot
therefore be " proved " by anything less than himself. All else can be just witness to him. Knowledge of him and about him must come directly
from him. This is what we mean by the inner conviction of the Holy Spirit. And this does not depend
on our having some psychological pre-requisite in the
shape of a capacity for belief.

We might note here that the various Christian
communities have tended to emphasize one or other
of these credentials above the rest. There are some
who would rest the grounds of their faith wholly in
the Church, conceived of as the infallible source of
all true doctrine. Others would bind themselves
to the letter of Scripture as their sole authority.
Others again would maintain that an inner light of
the Spirit guides them, and they need no other norm.
This book is written out of the conviction that all
three credentials are needed and that they are
mutually illuminating. The Church, unless subject to the authority of Scripture, may wander far
from the facts on which she was founded. The
Bible, read in isolation from the Church's tradition
and life, can be made to yield an infinite number of
new " religions ", each claiming to be a fresh

revelation to mankind. Personal experience, exalted into the sole credential of Christianity, leads to a hopelessly subjective interpretation of the Faith. The three credentials belong together: and they speak together of Christ.

It might be best and simplest to say that Christ himself is *the* credential of the Christian Faith. It is he that the Church trusts and worships. It is of him that the Bible speaks. It is the living Christ that the Christian knows in his inner life. Hence to understand the meaning of the Christian Faith, and to elucidate its content, it is best to begin with him.

For further reading:

"Christian Apologetics": Alan Richardson.
"Christian Faith and Natural Science": Karl Heim.

CHAPTER II

JESUS CHRIST

EVERY student of religion knows what a tremendous impression has been made by a relatively small number of great leaders and teachers. One might reasonably expect that this kind of personal impact would be most noticeable in the more primitive and locally confined religions and that it would tend to disappear in the more developed faiths with universal pretensions. We could understand that one man could make a deep and lasting influence on the thoughts and practices of a particular tribe or people, and even draw to himself a kind of worship; but we should expect that a world-religion would be emancipated from such personal ties and express its faith in terms of general principles and symbols. Yet the facts are otherwise. Primitive and local religions, as far as we know them, speak of powers and influences normally unrelated to any historic personage, while the great world-faiths (and they are not many) are concretely and unmistakably related to the figures of the Buddha, Moses, Christ, and Mohammed. No one seriously wanting to understand any of these religions, which between them have affected the lives of the majority of the human race, could possibly ignore the personality and influence of these leaders and founders. However much we must allow for later development or deviation, we must first of all reckon with these historic figures and try to penetrate into the secret of their abiding influence.

Even the most superficial observation will show us,
however, that the relationship of these faiths to the
historic figures with which they have been associated
varies considerably. The Buddha (Gautama) is the
most elusive of these founders for the modern
historian, and his influence among Buddhists is that
of his traditional teaching more than his person.
Moses stands out clearly as an historical figure of
importance in Jewish history and religion, but no
Jew would tolerate the idea that he was in any sense
the *founder* of their religion. Mohammed is the
supreme prophet of the Muslim world and his
teaching the supreme authority, but no kind of
divine honour is paid to him nor is he regarded as a
" Saviour ". The relationship of Christ to Christianity is quite other. It is central to the faith—
intimate, personal, permanent, and living. Only of
the Christian faith could it be said that if the founding personality were dissolved into myth the religion
itself would collapse, leaving, no doubt, an enduring
ethical and spiritual influence but no trace of the
driving and controlling impulse that has changed
world history during the last two thousand years.

What is it that makes the person of Christ so
decisively important in the Christian Faith? In the
answer to that question lies the heart of the Christian
message. For, as it has been often said, Christianity
is Christ. The Church in every century, in all its
forms, and in every place, has not only preserved
and propagated his teachings but has worshipped
him as a living Lord and paid him divine honour.
The individual Christian is related to him not simply
as a follower to a great historic leader but intimately
and personally, so that not only saints and mystics
but millions of ordinary men and women speak of

him and to him as a living person, claiming and seeking a close union with him that could best be described in terms of human friendship.

When we turn to the records of the New Testament we find that this emphasis on the person of Jesus Christ was there at the beginning. Whatever else we may believe about them, these books are clearly first-hand evidence about what the earliest Christians (many of them eye-witnesses of Jesus' own ministry) considered to be the essence of the faith. The convergence of their testimony to the supremacy of Christ and the new era that he inaugurated is all the more remarkable when we consider the wide variety of background and approach that is already apparent in the Church of the New Testament. We do not need to be critical scholars to notice the difference of language, culture, and religious ideas between such books as St. Mark's Gospel, St. John's Gospel, the epistles of St. Paul, the speeches in the Book of the Acts, the epistle of St. James, and the Book of Revelation—yet each of these in its own way speaks of Christ (the Christ whom most of them had known and seen in action) in staggering terms of religious awe and devotion and claims that in and through him God has acted uniquely and decisively in human history. The Christian Faith begins and ends with such belief in Christ.

Here are some of the things that are said by the different witnesses. " The beginning of the Gospel of Jesus Christ, the Son of God." [1] " These are written, that ye might believe that Jesus is the Christ, the Son of God; and that believing ye might have life through his name." [2] " That at the name of Jesus every knee should bow, of things in heaven,

[1] St. Mark i. 1.   [2] St. John xx. 31.

and things in earth, and things under the earth; and that every tongue should confess that Jesus Christ is Lord, to the glory of God the Father." [1] " God hath made that same Jesus, whom ye have crucified, both Lord and Christ." [2] " My brethren, have not the faith of our Lord Jesus Christ, the Lord of glory, with respect of persons." [3] " Unto him that loved us, and washed us from our sins in his own blood, and hath made us kings and priests unto God and his Father; to him be glory and dominion for ever and ever. Amen." [4]

These expressions of the uniqueness and supremacy of Jesus Christ could, of course, be multiplied from the pages of the New Testament. The full force of them has been softened for many of us by liturgical familiarity, but no one can miss the triumphant claim that is being made on behalf of one who, for their contemporaries, was simply one out of many victims of the religious–political situation in the province of Judæa. There is no comparable claim made for any other religious leader known to history. Christianity is based from the beginning on a belief that " Christ is Lord ". This is, in fact, believed to be the earliest form of Christian creed. To the modern man it is perhaps not immediately apparent what is meant by such an expression. It will be enough to say at this point that the New Testament Greek word for " Lord "—Kyrios—was contemporarily used not only to describe the dignity and powers of the Emperor but in the Greek translation of the Old Testament as the translation of " Jehovah ". To say that Jesus was " Lord " implied setting him at the centre of life, offering him

---

[1] Philippians ii. 10–11.   [2] Acts ii. 36.
[3] St. James ii. 1.   [4] Revelation i. 5–6.

the total obedience that the religious mind will give to God alone. From the beginning, then, there is implicit in the Christian claim an exaltation of Jesus Christ to nothing less than equality with God.

It is precisely this kind of claim for Jesus Christ that has been an obstacle to belief for many people otherwise well-disposed towards Christianity. Sometimes the claim is made so crudely, dogmatically, and indigestibly that it is little wonder that it is resented and resisted, and Christians would do well to remember that historically there has been more than one way of expressing the belief that Christ is Lord. Belief in the deity of Christ is not a kind of take-it-or-leave-it formula to be hurled at the head of an enquirer. It is a doctrine that has baffled the sharpest minds of the Church through the centuries to express in adequate words, and the truth that it enshrines is one that may well dawn slowly on the mind of a seeker on the Christian way. Yet for all its difficulty the paradox holds that the most daring and perplexing item in the Christian creed has been always at the centre of the Church's life. Nothing less than the belief that Christ is Lord and God has ever ultimately nourished the Christian community.

It is important to refer as often as possible to the New Testament statements about Christ and his significance for God and man. For the attempt has been made in past years by many a brilliant writer (and is still reflected by many less brilliant) to prove that this exaltation of the Christ was a development within the Church some time after the death of Jesus—who is supposed to have made no such impression on his contemporaries and to have taught a different kind of religion. It seems at first a plausible argument that Jesus appeared as a Jewish prophet with an unusually powerful message about God and the way men ought to live; and that subsequently, under the influence of the practices of the mystery-religions, and dominated by the theology of Paul, the Church transformed the simple prophetic message into an elaborate creed and the messenger into a Saviour-God. When this theory is cleverly expounded and invested with the authority of a scientific scholarship it finds an immediate echo in the heart of modern Western man who says: "This is just what I have suspected: I have always admired Jesus Christ and the kind of life he stood for, but I have no time for the mumbo-jumbo of the Church." And so, although the theory has long since lost serious theological support and would hardly be defended by the secular historian, there still exists a popular belief that the Christian Faith as expounded by the Churches is very different from the religion of Jesus.

The decisive factor in settling this question is the evidence of the New Testament. We may claim, if we like, that the New Testament books, being written from thirty to over a hundred years after the death of Jesus, have already deformed the teaching of the Master and given a false impression of his person. But we must admit that once we have rejected the evidence of the New Testament we are in the realm of sheer fantasy and speculation. For there is no other evidence on which to form an opinion. The method, then, that was adopted to support the conception of a " Jesus-religion " contrasted with the developed Christian Faith was that of a critical reshaping of the material of the Gospels. In this process " miracle" was eliminated, the Fourth Gospel dismissed, and every reference that resembled

Christian orthodox doctrine explained as a later addition of the Church. It is important to note that the answer to this critical handling of the Gospels was not (except in certain quarters) an indignant repudiation of the critical method as applied to the New Testament, but a stricter and better critical investigation. It is admitted by most Christian scholars today that the New Testament documents have come to us through normal human processes of interpretation and editing, and that there is evidence of development of doctrine within the New Testament itself. But the consensus of critical opinion has rejected the notion that we can discover behind the pages of the Gospels and Epistles another Jesus than the one in whom the apostles believed, and a simple ethical message uncontaminated by dogma. It is now recognized that those who strove to do so allowed subjective notions as to what *must* have taken place, or what *must* have been said, to dictate their conclusions as to the authenticity of particular texts. For instance, to approach the recorded story of Jesus with a nineteenth-century dogmatism as to what is possible in the physical world is neither scientific nor reasonable: and to construct from one's imagination a picture of Jesus acceptable to the pre-1914 world, and then to eliminate as " accretion " all that we find in the Gospels that is alien to this picture, is to make nonsense of historical investigation. The trend of recent criticism has been surely sounder. What is now sought is to know what indeed the apostles believed about Jesus; what can be known about his recorded teaching; and what the essence of the original Christian message really was.

The field of New Testament scholarship is too

vast for anyone to attempt to summarize its findings. And the investigation is still in process. But certain things can be confidently stated. It is no longer believed that we must date the New Testament books late into the second century and regard them as well beyond the horizon of the men who actually companied with Jesus. The epistles are mostly to be taken as first-hand evidence of the beliefs of the Church during the first generation of Christians, and the Gospels to be dated between thirty and seventy years after the Crucifixion, with evident background material that goes back to the contemporaries of Jesus. And when we attempt to use the most radical critical methods to reach back to the earliest strata of the tradition it is clear that at no point do we reach an " historic Jesus " who bears no resemblance to the Christ worshipped by the Church. In short, the result of the most stringent examination of the records shows us a Jesus acknowledged as Son of God, received as Saviour, and believed to be God's supreme and decisive Word to this world.

"Who am I?" All the Gospels agree that this was the critical question put by Jesus to all who came into contact with him. It was explicitly asked by him of the disciples on a particular occasion, and Peter gave the answer: " Thou art the Christ, the Son of the living God ".[1] As we can see from the Gospel story, this incident was a turning-point in Jesus' ministry: the recognition, whatever it involved, meant that he would now go through with the grim and glorious events that lay ahead. But the question is implicit in every encounter. Who is this man who " speaks with authority and not as the

[1] St. Matthew xvi. 16.

scribes "? "What manner of man is this, that
even the wind and sea obey him?" "Art thou the
Christ? tell us." "Art thou the King of the
Jews?" "Who is this Son of man?" The
Gospels are full of the astonishment and speculation
aroused by Jesus among the common people, the
Roman authorities, the Jewish religious leaders,
and his own intimate friends. And he himself,
quite unlike all those whom we are accustomed to
call "saints", seems to have encouraged this con-
centration upon his person. St. John's Gospel gives
us the tremendous series of "I am . . ." that seem
to echo the voice of the Old Testament Jehovah
("I AM THAT I AM") "I am the bread of life";
"I am the light of the world"; "I am the good
shepherd"; "I am the way, the truth, and the
life". But the other Gospels (known to scholars
as the "synoptic" Gospels because they present
the story from roughly the same "point of view")
give equally remarkable instances of this self-asser-
tion. We are familiar with the sound of the Sermon
on the Mount—"Ye have heard that it was said by
them of old time . . . but I say unto you" [1]—and
we miss the sense of shock which these words must
have given. It is as if a very young preacher were
to rise in a conference of the World Council of
Churches today and say: "The Bible says . . . but
_I_ say . . ." St. Matthew's Gospel gives another
instance of this unique emphasis in reporting the
familiar invitation: "Come unto me, all ye that
labour and are heavy laden, and I will give you
rest." [2] Transfer these words to the lips of any
other great historical character and you will be
conscious of their stupendous implications.

[1] St. Matthew v. 27.   [2] St. Matthew xi. 28.

No less bewildering to the ordinary man are the answers that he gave to the other question: " What am I doing? " Most great religious leaders, asked that question, would probably reply that they were showing a way of life or relaying a message from God. Jesus claimed to be doing both, but also to be doing much more. The Fourth Gospel reports the remark, " I am come that they might have life, and that they might have it more abundantly ",[1] and indicates that for Jesus this life-giving mission lay consciously behind the entire drama of his life, death, and resurrection. The events of the Passion-week, for instance, are clearly interpreted by him as a decisive crisis in human affairs. " Now is the judgment of this world: now shall the prince of this world be cast out." The synoptic Gospels give us exactly the same impression. " The Son of man is come to seek and to save that which was lost." [2] " The Son of man came not to be ministered unto, but to minister, and to give his life a ransom for many." [3] " This is my body which is given for you." " The Son of man is not come to destroy men's lives but to save them." [4] Behind all these sayings, and there are many more of this kind, there is an evident claim to be doing a unique work for mankind. The men who heard such words were under no illusions that he considered himself simply another in the line of prophets of Israel: they knew in the end that he spoke and acted with the authority of a unique divine intervention in human affairs. Otherwise, as we can see from the account of his trial, it is unlikely that he would have been crucified.

The Church, then, has not been dealing in

[1] St. John x. 10. St. Luke xix. 10.
[3] St. Matthew xx. 28. St. Luke ix. 56.

theological verbiage when proclaiming a Christ
who is more than a human religious leader. The
teaching of the Christian Faith about the person of
Jesus Christ may seem tough and logically intractable; the creeds and confessions may appear to
speak in metaphysical riddles; the average Christian
may become tongue-tied when asked what he means
by " his only Son, our Lord "; but all these com-
plications and hesitations are really attempts to do
justice to the facts. For the facts are not simple.
The impression made by Jesus Christ on mankind
has been of nothing less than a unique divine intervention. His questions of " Who am I? " and
" What am I doing? " are inescapable for anyone
who comes within his orbit. And when the answer
dawns on us it is not strange that for a unique
person and a unique event we cannot find simple,
logical words and phrases. In a sense the Church
has been struggling from the beginning to express
what his followers believe about their Lord. Words
have to be found, although no words are ever
adequate. The early centuries of Church history
are crammed with theological discussion about the
person of Christ. We should find most of it rather
tiresome reading today; yet the motive behind it
was sound. If Christ is to be proclaimed as world-
saviour we must try to speak of him in terms that do
justice to the facts. The difficulty, or even impossibility, of discovering an adequate formula is no
excuse for shirking the task, and the consensus of
Christian opinion has found in some of the definitions
of the early theologians statements that can at least
serve as the best approximations to the truth, if not
as infallible tests of orthodoxy. (" Orthodoxy " is
sometimes spoken of rather contemptuously, as if it

meant the abdication of the critical faculty. But in its etymological sense of " holding right opinions " it ought surely to be the aim of every reasonable man. And in fact the victory of orthodoxy in the Christian debate about the person of Christ meant nothing less than the spreading of " right opinions " about the most important matter we can have to decide— the one to whom we confide ourselves, body and soul.)

The Apostles' Creed speaks of " Jesus Christ his only Son our Lord, who was conceived by the Holy Ghost, born of the Virgin Mary, suffered under Pontius Pilate, was crucified, dead, and buried, he descended into hell; the third day he rose again from the dead, he ascended into heaven, and sitteth on the right hand of God the Father Almighty; from thence he shall come to judge the quick and the dead ".

This is an early attempt (although not as early as the apostles whose name has been attached to it) to state what Christians believe about their Lord. At first sight it raises a host of questions for the modern man. What is conception by the Holy Ghost? Why this mention of Pontius Pilate? Why is nothing said about the life and teaching? What kind of world is it in which a man descends, rises, ascends, and sits and comes to judge? To go into all these questions would require another book, or series of books; but we must here frankly admit that the Apostles' Creed, like the New Testament from which its assertions come, operates with a language and system of images that are no longer familiar—and can indeed be very misleading. Anyone who was honestly trying today to put into words and images that we can recognize the essential

Christian facts would have to use a different framework. The difficulty is not simply that we have a vastly enlarged and complicated picture of the universe, but that we have a prosaic and literalist approach to verbal statements. We tend to imagine, for instance, that we have now evolved far beyond the point of believing in a Christ who could actually sit down on a throne in a physically-located heaven; when it is certain that the compilers of the Creed meant no such thing by " sitteth on the right hand of God ". Expressions of that kind had a symbolic significance for the men who wrote them and read them which the modern Western cannot immediately grasp.

Yet probably too much has been made of these difficulties. We accept traditional phraseology in our everyday speech without continually explaining its scientific inaccuracy. If I were to say, " I saw the sun rise magnificently behind the Alpine peaks which were bathed in pink ", I should not expect an opponent to dismiss my statement as a tissue of lies because in fact it is not the sun that rises but the earth that revolves, or a friend to leap to my defence explaining that I did not literally mean that the Alps took a bath. It is about time that we learned to apply some similar common sense to the consideration and explanation of creeds and Bible. It does not really take a great effort of the imagination to reach the heart of what is being said in the traditional language of the Christian faith, however unfamiliar some of its expressions may be. Why, after all, should we expect the description of the unique and astounding act of God in human history to be couched in the language of the operation instructions for a television-set?

What, then, is the Apostles' Creed saying about Jesus Christ?

First, that he was a man. Today we find that something that hardly needs saying: we know that he was a man, existing like other men at a certain period in history; we know how to range him in the human pageant of historical characters, and are not likely to imagine that he was an apparition, demon, or demi-god. But it was otherwise when the Creed was composed. Influential bodies of opinion on the fringe of the Church held that Jesus only seemed to be a man, did not really die as men die. And still today we occasionally hear so-called "champions of orthodoxy" speak of the divinity of Christ in such unguarded terms as to suggest that they do not really believe in his humanity. Orthodoxy has become so bound up with believing in Christ's deity that we forget that there was a time when the prevalent heresy was to deny his real existence as a man.

The Creed is thus concerned to emphasize his humanity. He was born. By a strange reversal of history this statement of his normal human birth has been taken to express a defiant supernaturalism. But the supernatural is asserted of his conception, not his birth. Mary is called "Virgin" in reference to the supernatural conception, but the emphasis here is on real human birth. Christmas speaks of the birth of a baby as all babies are born. It is probable that the compilers of the Creed were more anxious to defend the faith against those who denied his natural birth than those who denied his supernatural conception.

He suffered and died as do all human beings. The words "under Pontius Pilate" anchor this suffering and dying in a precise harbour of human history. The Christian faith is thus preserved against any mythologizing of the person of its Lord. He was not a mere divine influence or emanation: it is not the " Christ-idea " that Christians worship. " We have heard . . . we have seen with our eyes . . . we have looked upon . . . our hands have handled ", says the apostle. Whatever else may be believed about Jesus Christ, the Church holds that he existed as a man—a real man.

The reality of Jesus as a man has been often obscured by an exaggerated piety or a misplaced reverence. We have seen how impossible it is to construct from the Gospels a " biography " of Jesus from which all elements of the supernatural have been removed; but this should not blind us to the pure humanity that shines through the pages of the Gospels. We are not reading there of a God pretending to be a man, nor of a psychological monstrosity who switched humanity and divinity on and off according to the requirements of the moment. We meet one who walked and talked, hungered and thirsted, and " was in all points tempted like we are, yet without sin ". Only in this last—" yet without sin "—does he transcend the humanity we know, but even here we instinctively recognize him as truly human, more truly human than we are—for this is man as we know he ought to be. Jesus Christ is revealed in the Gospels as Man. It was his favourite description of himself (the expression " Son of man " has this sense in the original Aramaic which he spoke). And the New Testament speaks of him as the representative man, the one in whom our humanity finds its true expression.

Secondly, the Scriptures and the Church speak of

him as " Son of God ". " His only Son our Lord."
It is this unique status of Jesus Christ that we have
seen to be the central emphasis of all the New Testament writers. What is actually being said? The
phrases used in the Bible and in Christian theology—
" Son of God ", " Word Incarnate ", " Christ ",
" Lord ", " Saviour "—are all attempts to express
a unique relationship to God, and all are capable
of being misinterpreted and misunderstood. We
might clear the ground by noting what is *not* being
said. It is not asserted that Jesus was a man who
was so good that God decided to " adopt " him as his
special son. On the contrary, the evidence (and
not only in the Fourth Gospel) is that the relationship is eternal. Jesus Christ " comes " from the
Father. " In the beginning was the Word." On
the other hand, it is not asserted that Jesus was
simply God on earth with all the divine attributes,
as it were pretending to be man. No one reading
the Gospels could get the impression that the throne
of the universe had been vacated for a period of
thirty years, or that God died upon a cross. Nor is
it being said that at one moment Jesus Christ acted
as God and at another as a man.

It is significant that the whole history of the
attempts to describe the unique person of Christ
within the Church has been more concerned with
denying such errors as these than with finding an
agreed positive statement. For it is clear that no
completely satisfactory statement can be found in
human words for a unique event. Our words have
their origin in the things we know and are familiar
with in our daily conversation. If a unique event
has occurred it is natural that we have difficulty in
discovering current words and phrases to express it.

The best that we can do is to follow the example of the New Testament and use the language of imagery. If we look at two of the commonest images we shall perhaps come nearest to the truth.

The expression " Son of God " suggests that we find a parallel in the human relationship of son to father. A son reflects his father—not automatically as a glass reflects our face—but in the freedom of a response of love and obedience. If we were to try to imagine a perfect father and a perfect son the relationship would be one of practical identity. The Bible teaching is that all men are summoned to be " sons of God " in this sense—that is, to reflect him in love and obedience. But it speaks of only one who has made this perfect response; only one who reveals the absolute relationship. And it indicates that this relationship is an eternal one, so that when Jesus appeared on earth this fact can be described in the words : " God sent his Son ". The Son, then, is God's other self—to put it in crude language, " all of God that can be expressed in human terms ".

The other helpful image is that of the Word of God. A word is an expression of ourselves, a means of communication. It is by words that I am attempting to convey to you not only ideas that are in my mind, but something of my own self. A God who communicates with men, a God who gives himself in this way, is a God who speaks, who utters a Word. This is a common conception in the Old Testament, and it is in this sense that we are to understand the phrase : " The Word of God came to . . ." The Fourth Gospel begins with a use of this familiar conception to explain the nature of the coming of Jesus. " The Word ", we read, " was made flesh, and dwelt among us." God, in other words, expressed himself to man—not just through prophets and teachers as in the Old Testament—but uniquely in taking human flesh and blood. This is the meaning of the term " incarnation "—i.e. becoming flesh. We shall see later how this " becoming flesh " dominates the entire Christian conception of God and his relation to the world. Here we are concerned with it as a way of understanding the person of Jesus Christ. He was man, but in him "dwelleth all the fulness of the Godhead bodily".[1] The origin of Jesus, then, is utterly divine. This is God appearing on earth, but God, as has been said, stripped of all the divine attributes except that of love.

We might express the two poles between which our thoughts must move on this central doctrine of the Christian faith in some such way as this. Jesus Christ is divine: he is our God to whom we can pray. Jesus Christ is human; when he was on earth his own prayers were real.

Whatever stage we have reached in our own apprehension of this Christian affirmation, we are bound to recognize that Christianity does depend on our answer to this question: Who am I? We may reject all the formulations of Christian doctrine, but, if we are serious in our quest, we are driven back again and again to the evidence of the Gospels. And there we are confronted with the Lord who was seen and known to be man, and yet who acted with all the authority of God.

It is from our understanding of this unique claim that we can go forward to examine what the Christian Faith has to say about the being and purposes

[1] Colossians ii. 9.

of God. For it is illusion to suppose that we have already a satisfactory notion of God into which we must fit whatever we learn from Jesus Christ. Rather would it be true to say that what we know about God we have learned, directly or indirectly, from Jesus Christ. " Philip saith unto him, Lord, shew us the Father, and it sufficeth us. Jesus saith unto him, Have I been so long time with you, and yet hast thou not known me, Philip? he that hath seen me hath seen the Father." [1]

For further reading:

" Jesus of Nazareth ": Bishop Gore.
" The Riddle of the New Testament ": Hoskyns and Davey.

---

[1] St. John xiv. 8–9.

CHAPTER III

THE DISCLOSURE OF GOD

THE familiar ending of a Christian prayer is " through Jesus Christ our Lord ". If we pause to consider why this formula should be used we shall find that, far from being a kind of pious postscript to a God-directed petition, it expresses what ought to be the inspiring and controlling belief behind the prayer. For the use of Jesus' name is decisive. It not only rules out petitions that are inconsistent with our knowledge of his character (could we pray : " God, mutilate my enemy through Jesus Christ our Lord "?) but it also clearly reveals how we come to God and how God comes to us. The Christian approach to God, and God's approach to the Christian, is always " through Jesus Christ our Lord ".

This is why we have begun our study of the Christian Faith with the encounter with Jesus Christ. It is, of course, possible to begin with the doctrine of God and then to proceed to consider the teaching of the Church about Jesus Christ. But this method presents certain serious difficulties. In the first place, it would be impossible to describe the Christian doctrine of God without immediately including what we have learned " through Jesus Christ our Lord ". And in the second place it would be difficult to avoid giving the impression that the Christian has somehow access to information about God into which what we learn " through Jesus Christ our Lord " has somehow to be fitted. Many of our difficulties in accepting the orthodox view of the divinity of Christ arise from thus beginning at the wrong point. If we think we know already who God is we may have the greatest trouble in making Jesus Christ fit into the picture. But when we see how, for us, the picture begins with Jesus Christ the problem is no longer the same. For the question is then not: How can Jesus Christ be God? but: Who *is* this God who comes to me through Jesus Christ our Lord?

We begin, then, our understanding of the Christian doctrine of God with the person of Jesus Christ. This is how in fact we have received our knowledge of God. All our training in these matters has come to us in the context of the Christian Church and the Christian Scriptures. The God to whom we have been taught to pray, if we have been taught at all, is the God and Father of Jesus Christ. It would not be possible for us to think back to a time when we had a knowledge of God divorced altogether from Jesus Christ. And when we try, as probably everybody does, to form some kind of picture of God in our minds the content is supplied, consciously or unconsciously, by what we have learned of Jesus Christ.

At this point, however, the question must arise: Does the Christian Faith, then, demand that we deny the validity of all other religions, and regard all knowledge of God among those who have never heard of Jesus, or reject his claim, as sheer illusion? There are some Christians who feel forced to adopt this attitude, but the great majority of theologians in all ages and sections of the Church have rejected it, and few sensitive Christians could be satisfied with a system of dogma that led to this conclusion.

In the first place, it is surely presumptuous for any mortal to limit the power of God to reveal himself to anyone he chooses. In the second place, no one who has really got to know a devout Muslim, Hindu, or Buddhist would find it possible to say that they had absolutely no knowledge of the true God, unless they were rigidly held in the blinkers of dogmatic prejudice. In the third place, most of us would find it impossible to ignore the evidence that children, before they have heard anything about Jesus Christ, show obvious signs of a knowledge of God. And in the fourth place, the entire Old Testament is a witness to the dealings of the living God with his people before the Incarnation happened.

The Christian belief that we know God " through Jesus Christ our Lord " is literally true for all who have been born within the confines of Christendom. But when we see the true meaning of this we shall find that it does not lead to a denial of any knowledge of God outside this fold. The New Testament does not speak of a sudden appearance of God for the first time—as if there were no connection between the God now revealed in Jesus Christ and the God of Abraham, Isaac, and Jacob. What the apostles are saying is: Behold, here is God, the God who has never left himself " without a witness ", fully revealed in Jesus Christ his Son. " Whom therefore ye ignorantly worship," said St. Paul to the Athenians, " him declare I unto you." [1] The apostles do not speak as if contact with God began abruptly with Jesus; nor do they imply that God became a different being when the clock struck A.D. They speak of a disclosure of what has been eternally true: *This* is God; from the beginning he is the

[1] Acts xvii. 23.

outgoing, seeking, saving God. The Incarnation is not an after-thought: it discloses what God is always and everywhere—the Father who reveals himself through the Son. " In the beginning was the Word . . ."

When we insist that God is known " through Jesus Christ our Lord " we are not setting up " our religion " as the truth and relegating all others to the realms of falsehood and superstition. We are simply saying that the man who has met God in Jesus Christ recognizes him as the God of all nations and religions, " the true light that lighteth every man that cometh into the world ". We might put it this way: the Christian Faith does not say that there is no knowledge of God outside a conscious belief in Christ, but it does say that wherever a man has a knowledge of God, it is because God has revealed himself, a revelation that is perfected in the incarnation of Jesus Christ.

Christian belief speaks of God as a person. Only a personal God could reveal himself in human flesh and blood. But not only the New Testament speaks in these personal terms: the Old Testament is very clearly the record of the personal dealings of God with men. Indeed, this is one of the difficulties that modern men find in the Bible—the bluntly human personal language that is used to describe the actions of God. Sceptics in every age have delighted to draw attention to the God who walks and talks, is pleased or angry, kind or violent. And Christians have not been slow to come forward with their apologies for the " primitive strata " in the Biblical revelation. The criticisms and explanations, however, miss the point. The Biblical records, at every period of their composition, are concerned not with the formulations of exact philosophical definitions of God's nature but with a vital conversation between man and God. The relationship between man and God—a working relationship, not a theory—is the theme of the Bible. And such a relationship, a conversation, must be in contemporary human terms. When we read, for instance, that " God said, Let us make man in our image " we are obviously not to imagine that such a sentence was actually spoken at some precise point in the stratosphere and overheard for the record by some mystic scribe. Nor are we dealing fairly by the Bible if we simply note that this was a conception of God prevalent in the school of Semitic theology at the time of the Babylonian Exile. We are in the presence of an encounter between God and man in which God is active and personal. It matters comparatively little where and when this encounter was recorded: it must in any case be recorded in the language of the writer and his times. What matters supremely is that millions since have overheard this conversation and heard in their own hearts the echoes of a living God, speaking of *their* relationship to him.

Once again we have to be on our guard against feeling too superior to the writers of past ages. When Hebrew scribes wrote of God's " right arm " they were even less likely to have any literal understanding of the words in their minds than we are. Vivid, picturesque speech of this kind is natural to the Eastern mind—and natural to the language of intimate religion in almost any age and land. It is perhaps only to our unimaginative, materialist age that it is necessary to issue the warning that when we say that God is a " person " we do not mean that he has arms and legs. By affirming " personality " of God the Christian Faith is concerned that we talk about the Deity in the highest terms we know.

There is a prevalent opinion that such " personalist " terms are unworthy of a pure religion, still more of a religion claiming any kind of finality. It is, perhaps, necessary to emphasize that the word " person " applied to God is an inadequate description. There are elements in human personality which are incompatible with divinity. But it is difficult to see what other term can be used. For if we are anxious to think of God in the highest terms available to us we are forced to use the language of personal qualities. It is strange that so many modern writers and speakers assume that it is somehow more intellectually respectable to deny to divinity the qualities that are most personal—the ability to think, plan, create, and love. The Christian God cannot be described merely in terms of abstract force or influence. Above all, he is one with whom we can have personal relations. If we are to conceive at all of a God who is responsible for all that exists, then it is hard to see how, for instance, the human quality of love can have come from a being who is himself incapable of loving.

It is remarkable how silent the Bible is about the being of God. Anyone who comes to it with the idea that, as a religious book, it must be full of direct teaching about God's nature and properties will be sadly disappointed, and may rightly conclude that it is not, in this sense, a religious book at all. Neither the Old Testament nor the New contains much in the way of systematic thought about the being of God. They record actions, encounters between men and God. The Bible is very largely the account of things that happened. On the basis of these happenings theologians have drawn up their doctrines about God's nature and man's, but the primary emphasis in Biblical faith is on the living encounter of God and man. Reflection upon it is a secondary activity.

From this it follows that the Christian Faith does not, any more than the Bible, begin with arguments about God's existence. The Bible is the record of men who met with God, and who would never for a moment have thought of trying to justify a belief in his existence by rational proofs. And the Christian Faith begins with a living encounter of men with God in Christ—an encounter which makes such attempts equally irrelevant. Beginning with this primary encounter theologians and others have sought to make their faith rationally intelligible to others, and in the course of this attempt have elaborated arguments about God's existence which may, or may not, have validity in the eyes of the unbeliever; but the Christian Faith is chiefly concerned with the statement: This is what God has done, is doing, and will do.

The basic Christian doctrine of God is therefore that of a " living God "—a God who is active in the world that he has made. In this the Christian Faith is radically separated from all religions which teach a static God, and from all philosophies or theosophies which speak in terms of First Cause, Principle of Being, or Divine Essence. Christians believe in a God who is busy in his world, and is known in his acts. He is a sovereign God, not bound by fatalistic law; he is a living God, not an abstract principle; he is a God with a purpose, not a prisoner in a cosmic drama, without beginning, end, or meaning.

Thus, when the Christian says " I believe in God " he is speaking about a living relationship with a person. If this is understood a great many of the difficulties associated with religious debate disappear. For personal relationships are very different from our relationship with things or ideas. The statement " I know John Smith " has quite other implications than the statement " I know this house " or " I know that two and two make four ". Believing in John Smith is the result of a personal encounter. It involves also belief in John Smith as an object in space and belief in the " Idea " of John Smith, but fundamentally the statement rests on a two-way traffic in communication between me and him. Belief in the Christian God rests fundamentally on such a communication. It involves the idea of God's " existence " (although not as an object in space), but "existence" as such is not a very helpful term. To believe in God is to have met him, to be met by him, and anything that we find ourselves able to say about his nature derives from this encounter.

Most of the classic confessions of the Church attempt some description of the nature of God. The Shorter Catechism answers the question What is God? " God is a Spirit, infinite, eternal, and unchangeable, in his being, wisdom, power, holiness, justice, goodness, and truth." Such an attempt to reflect on the content of the Christian encounter is legitimate and useful, provided we remember that God is not an " object " to be described. " Le Dieu défini est le Dieu fini " (God defined is God finished). A God who can be encompassed within the human mind is clearly not God. A God who is an object to be discovered and described is equally not God. This is why we cannot turn to the pages of the Bible and read off a neat description of the total attributes of God. Language about the Christian God, like the language of love, is image, metaphor, poetry, music: when it becomes scientifically descriptive the virtue goes out of it.

Why, then, it may be asked, have Christians elaborated a theology? Why have they written books " about God "? Why do they publish confessions of faith and creeds? The answer is that we must occasionally use language that is as accurately descriptive as we can make it in order to clarify our thinking and to safeguard the Christian inheritance. For although no descriptions of God can be adequate, there are those which are true to the Christian encounter and those which are manifestly false. It will be sufficient for our purpose to select one familiar Christian statement and to see how it seeks to describe the God who meets us in Jesus Christ.

" I believe in God the Father Almighty." Here we have an attempt at description in the shortest possible phrase. The controlling Christian word for God is " Father ", and when we think through the implications of the use of this particular word we shall have come nearest to an understanding of what Christians mean by " God ". But first of all we ought to look at this adjective " almighty ".

A vast number of problems loom up whenever we approach the subject of divine omnipotence. Quite apart from the trick questions (" Can God make a stone so heavy that he can't lift it? ") the very nature of the world as we know it seems to challenge the existence of a God who is both good and almighty. This is the classic dilemma—as old as the Christian Faith: either God is good and not almighty, or he is almighty and not good. There is no swift answer to this dilemma, except to note where it arises. It arises out of the problem of evil. What sensitive soul has never felt that some particular evil seems to call in question either God's power or his love? Now for the existence of evil in the world there seems to be no adequate reason. And no religion or philosophy has ever explained its origin. Evil is a fact we must recognize; and as a fact it defies our rational equipment. Christianity offers no theoretical answer to evil—only, what is more important —a practical one. But it is asserted with all confidence and power that the one final arbiter of all things, including human destiny, is Almighty God. The God who meets us in Christ is a God who is without a rival on the throne. He can do whatever he wills to do: there is no kind of evil that is ultimately intractable in his hand. With this assertion the Christian Faith, while recognizing that the existence of evil is an irrational element in our thinking, utterly repudiates the view that God may be at the mercy of some enemy power.

The other chief problem that haunts this idea of omnipotence is that of our free-will. Here again we meet a question that no religion or philosophy has been able to solve—how to reconcile our evident (though limited) free-will with the timeless knowledge and control of an almighty God, or of a deterministic law. There is no use spending time with this question. For discussion about any kind of determinism is by its very nature futile. If we have no free-will at all, then our arguments are meaningless: they are merely pre-determined noises that we make: there can be no such thing as truth. When we come up against this full-stop the only thing we can do is to recognize two truths that we are not able fully to reconcile. And this the Christian does by asserting that God is almighty—and yet not responsible for the evil that we choose. This paradox holds right through the Christian Faith— that God is all in all, yet that we have the possibility of defying him; that God does all for our salvation, and yet we are free to respond or not, and in this sense everything depends on our response. There is no way of avoiding this kind of dilemma, either by denying God's omnipotence or the reality of our free-will. Nor do we avoid it by rejecting the Christian Faith in favour of some other religion or philosophy. All that we can say is that there is a Christian answer which, in the testimony of millions, works in practice.

By saying that God is almighty we are not spinning theories about divinity but attempting to describe what is disclosed in our encounter with Jesus Christ. He speaks of his Father as one who is " perfect ", without whom not a sparrow can fall to the ground, who " knoweth what things ye have need of, before ye ask him ".[1]   He fully accepted the Old Testament picture of the absolute sovereignty and power of God. The Father disclosed by the Son is one who is wholly able to do what he wills to do, and from whose judgment there is no appeal.

If this were all we were able to say about the disclosure of God in Jesus Christ it would be important, but not distinctive. Jews and Muslims also believe in God's omnipotence. There is little value in the doctrine as a merely theoretical attribute of divinity. Its importance for the Christian arises in the context of the relationship of the universe, and of ourselves, to God. There are roughly three ways in which we can think of God as related to the universe.

(1) We can identify God with the universe, and

[1] St. Matthew vi. 8.

simply say that he *is* the sum total of all that exists—
or that all that exists *is* God. To this the Christian
says: the God in whom I believe is present everywhere in the universe, so that all things depend on
him—but in his omnipotence he does not depend on
the universe. It is he who has brought it into being
and sustains it from moment to moment. The
pantheist, who identifies God and the universe, must
simply worship all that is—whether good or evil.
The Christian believes that only the almighty God
is to be worshipped, and so distinguishes the creation
from the Creator.

> " Though earth and man were gone,
>   And suns and universes ceased to be,
>   And Thou wert left alone,
>   Every existence would exist in Thee."

(2) We can regard God and the universe as rival
powers. There have been those in every age who
try to solve the problem of evil by assigning the
universe to another god. Sometimes it has been
bluntly stated that creation itself is evil and that good
can only triumph when matter disappears and only
spirit remains. Sometimes a dualism is established
by which an equal struggle is conceived between the
good God and an evil power to whom the world
belongs. Sometimes the attempt is made to think
away the material universe as an illusion, leaving the
only reality a pure spirit. In a hundred different
ways inside and outside Christendom the omnipotence of God has been denied by such conceptions.
And it is surprising how easily a fundamental doubt
as to the almightiness of God can creep into even
devout Christian thinking. To believe in God, the
Father *almighty*, means that ultimately there is no

rival power—neither human nor satanic, economic nor atomic. Everything is completely within the competence of almighty God.

(3) We are left with the Christian conception of a universe created by, and utterly dependent on, God. This is why the Apostles' Creed follows the statement of God's omnipotence with " maker of heaven and earth ". The Christian Faith is not really concerned with the processes of this making. To repeat this item of the Creed is not to commit ourselves to some scientifically untenable theory of physical origins. It is an affirmation that the universe is neither God nor the possession of a rival god, but owes its origin to the Creator-God. We do not seek to discover God within the gaps of scientific knowledge, as if he could be invoked as an explanation when normal methods had broken down. We affirm that God is the reason why anything is at all, from the first moment of time to the present second when you are reading this line. " It is of the Lord's mercies that we are not consumed."

We naturally come then to ask what kind of a relationship there is between an almighty God and his universe, and in particular the human race to which we belong. The Christian Faith, out of the entire field of metaphor and imagery that is open here (and to express such a relationship metaphor is indispensable), without hesitation chooses this one—Father. "I believe in God the *Father* almighty."

Before we try to think out the implications of the Father-relationship with the human race we might want to ask if this has any meaning for the universe as a whole. The answer must surely be that we are now dealing with the primary concern of the Christian faith—the relationship between God and

c

man—and any statements about God's relationship to the whole universe must be secondary, and largely speculative. We are deriving our knowledge of God from our encounter with Jesus Christ, and that encounter is between God and man. We can indeed say that we learn from it that this is God's world, and catch the suggestion that all creation springs from a creative fatherly love, but in the thought-defying universe disclosed to us by modern science we can hardly make dogmatic statements as to how God is related to the whole. The Christian believes that nothing from the most infinitesimal flutter of an electron to the ultimate reaches of space-time lies outside the control of God almighty, but it is quite beyond our powers to say how God may be related to other beings or entities beyond our ken. We have to begin with ourselves: and for man his Word is Christ. Hence we keep to the God/man relationship and seek to understand what concerns us most. This is by no means to assert that God is concerned only with this one race on a planet which is an infinitesimal fraction of even the tiny fragment of the universe that has been disclosed. We cannot categorically deny that he has fatherly relations with other creatures beyond our ken. We do not know. But, after all, it is man who has discovered the immensities of the universe, and it is not unreasonable to believe that the greatest discovery of all may be his relationship to the God who is all in all. Christians believe that such a discovery is due to the revelation made in Jesus Christ.

What is meant by saying that God is Father is that the relationship suggested by father-and-son is the nearest human analogy we can find to the relationship of God to his human creatures. We are so accustomed to hearing of God as Father that the implications tend to be forgotten. We come to think of this as a natural and inevitable way of talking about God, whereas it is in fact the specifically *Christian* way of speaking and is closely bound up with the belief in Christ as Son of God. No other religion specifically employs this picture as its controlling conception of God. God is thought of as King, as Lord, as Power, as Influence, as Mystery, as Fate, as Terror, as a Shepherd. Christianity alone, on the authority of Jesus, proclaims that the supreme and significant name for God is Father. This is the meaning of the statement: " No man cometh unto the *Father* but by me."

In some ways this is one of the most astonishing things that Jesus constantly taught—that we should regard God as Father. For in his teaching there is no softening of the contrast between a holy God and a sinful human race. God is perfect; we are evil. There is no scaling-down of the Old Testament demands made upon men. Every time he says: " Ye have heard that it was said by them of old time . . . but I say unto you " there followed, not an easier claim but an infinitely harder one. And God remains the judge to whom we must all render an account. Yet through all, and above all, he insists that the name for God is Father for all who become his disciples. This implies that our relationship to God is more nearly described in terms of the love of a father and the trust of a son than in any other way. Such a thought controls the entire Christian conception of God.

If we think of an ideal relationship between parent and child it is surely one where on the one side there is love rather than mere power, and on the other trust rather than fear. Even in our experience that may fall far short of the ideal we can still see that this is a different sort of relationship from that of a master to his slave, and still more different from that of a manufacturer to his product. Yet these are alternative ways of thinking about God and the human race. When, for instance, we hear the complaint " Why does God not stop the war? (the strike? the slums?) " we are really listening to an implied desire to be slaves and not sons. For if God were to intervene at all points to ensure that his will alone be done, then he would cease to be Father. And when we hear the suggestion that God should have made us all perfect in the first place, this is really a demand that we should be merely the perfect products of a divine manufacturer. It is strange that the very people who assume that God is a kind of Father are often the first to demand that he should act as if he were not.

There is thus implied in the idea of divine father-hood two fundamental truths about man—freedom and responsibility. Because the Christian believes in God as Father he does not feel himself a mere puppet in his hands. Like a child, he can say Yes or No to the Father. Like a child, he is aware, how-ever dimly, of his responsibility in saying No. How-ever many problems are left unsolved by this way of thinking about God, it is recognizable by us as nearer to the truth about our situation than any rival theory. To call God Father means to be a *man*—and not a puppet or a slave.

We can now hazard a guess about the answer to the question that haunts mankind—why such beings as we are should ever have appeared. We can believe that God the Father wished to have something more than the automatic obedience of a created world, and so brought into being (just when, just how, does not matter) creatures who were free to respond to him, and to reflect something of his love, his thought, his beauty, and his creative power. The Bible throughout speaks of this purpose of God to nurture this human family, freely responding to him in fellowship and love. To believe in God the Father means to believe in mankind made, not as mere animal, but "in his image"—that is, capable of reflecting his being, as a son reflects a father.

When we come later to consider the heart of the Gospel—the way in which God rescues man from the predicament he is in through sin (saying No, and ceasing to reflect the Father)—we shall see again how it stems from the Fatherhood of God. For as God creates man with freedom and responsibility he does not rob him of them when he goes wrong. Therefore the rescuing action comes about not through force but through love. Before we go on to consider this central tenet of the Christian Faith we should pause to reconsider how the belief in God as Father is grounded in Jesus Christ his Son.

It is not simply a question of his teaching. He unmistakably taught his followers to call God Father. He spoke of his own Father continually— sometimes in the intimate Aramaic term that has been preserved for us, Abba. He taught his disciples to pray: Our Father. He used the argument of a father/son relationship in many forms. And he told the story of the Prodigal Son. This contains the essence of the Christian teaching about God the Father in his relationship to men. Man is a son— but a lost son in a far country. So long as all goes well he can forget the Father and please himself.

But when " he comes to himself ", having lost the support of the world, he remembers the Father. And the Father sees him " afar off " and runs to meet him: so he is restored to the bosom of the family. Here is divine fatherhood in action: love, and love alone, is the controlling power, and that which draws the son home. And trust, trust expressed in the words " I will arise and go to my father ", is the means by which the son responds. This is God the Father almighty in action.

This teaching of Jesus about God cannot be isolated from his person. He spoke of the seeking Father, but he himself came " to seek and to save that which was lost ".[1] He spoke of the character of the Father, but when asked, " Show us the Father ", he replied, " He that hath seen me hath seen the Father." [2] He spoke of " knowing the Father " but, instead of suggesting that this was a natural and obvious gift for all men, he said: " All things are delivered unto me of my Father: and no man knoweth the Son, but the Father; neither knoweth any man the Father, save the Son, and he to whomsoever the Son will reveal him." [3] These words (and there are many others that could be appositely quoted) surely mean that the disclosure of God the Father is through Jesus Christ his Son. The curious expression " only-begotten Son " indicates that Christ is Son as no other can be. Here is the perfect expression of the Father, the perfect reflection, the perfect image of God. In him God is wholly disclosed, as wholly disclosed as he can be to man. It is " through Jesus Christ, his Son our

[1] St. Luke xix. 10.
[2] St. John xiv. 9.
[3] St. Matthew xi. 27.

Lord, that we come to know God the Father almighty, maker of heaven and earth ".

For further reading:

"The Christian Apprehension of God": H. R. Mackintosh.

"Our Faith": Emil Brunner.

CHAPTER IV

THE DELIVERANCE OF MAN

IT would be possible to speak about the Christian Faith in such a way as to give the impression that it was simply a method of believing in God. This is the temptation of the intellectual. In sermon, discussion, and debate we try to isolate the " problem of God " and ask how Christianity brings a solution. Ways are suggested for approaching God, for inspiring belief, and the Gospel is sometimes presented as a kind of technique for inserting God into our thought-processes. From what we have seen of the Biblical disclosure of God it will be plain that Christianity has nothing to do with this intellectualist approach. The Bible is concerned with the living God, who makes himself known to us, very much more than with our methods of approach. The Bible has nothing to say about the " idea of God ". In the Bible God is known in his actions. And this is also the instinctive response of the ordinary man or woman. After all, it is not some theory about God that matters; but a living contact with One who not only exists but is really present to us all—a God who is active.

Christianity therefore has even more to say about what God does than who he is. That is why history plays a prominent part in the Christian Faith. Other religions and cults may speak in abstract terms about " spirituality ", the divine, immortality, the inner life, hidden truths. The Christian creeds speak of what has happened—Christ was born, suffered, died, rose, ascended. We inevitably find statements of abstract truth in the Bible and in the theology and preaching of the Church, but these are always tied to facts of history. The expression " God is love " rests on the historical statement that : " God so loved the world, that he gave his only-begotten Son, that whosoever believeth in him should not perish, but have everlasting life." [1] When we turn to the background of the Christian Faith for which our authority is the Old Testament we find again that truths about God are not disclosed in abstraction but come through his acts. That is why most of the Old Testament is history; and it is significant that in the Hebrew language " word " and " act " are not distinguished. We cannot understand the Christian Faith until we see how it is based throughout on the action of God—what he has done, is doing, and will do.

The question, then, that Jesus asked, " Who am I ? " is not a metaphysical question to be answered in terms of substances and essences. The reply which he accepted was: " Thou art the Christ ", and this refers to what he *does*. Even the expressions " Son of God " and " Son of Man " are not merely descriptive of his person as revealing the nature of God and the true nature of man. " For this purpose the Son of God was manifested, that he might destroy the works of the devil ",[2] we read; and " the Son of man is come to seek and to save that which was lost ".[3] And there are other words commonly used in the New Testament and the Church which indicate even more clearly the importance of what he does. " Saviour ", " Redeemer ", " Messiah ", " Healer ", " Victor " are

[1] St. John iii. 16.   [2] I John iii. 8.   [3] St. Luke xix. 10.

some of the titles which indicate the profound Christian conviction that he did not only reveal God to us but did something for the whole of mankind. The World Council of Churches has adopted as a kind of " minimum creed " for admission of member Churches the formula of acceptance of " Jesus Christ as God and Saviour ". By this the two-fold significance is recognized: that we find God fully revealed to us in Christ, and that this revelation is a " saving revelation "—in other words, he does something for us. Jesus Christ is thus both the discloser of God and the deliverer of man. He is, if you like, both God's way to man and man's way to God.

The question has here to be faced: does man need to find a way to God? Does man need a deliverer? There was a time, not so long ago, when any exponent of the Christian Faith would have had to spend some time arguing the relevance of a Gospel for a fallen world. The world was believed to be almost automatically on the up and up, and the Christian doctrine of sin seemed a lamentable hangover from a superstitious age. Today it hardly seems necessary to demonstrate that there is something wrong with humanity. The pendulum has swung so far that the late H. G. Wells, who spoke in his earlier works with the optimism of a triumphant humanist, wrote in his last book of mankind at the end of its tether. And it is remarkable that at least one philosophical writer of recent years has confessed that it was a growing conviction as to the truth of Original Sin that brought him to an acceptance of the Christian Faith. On every hand, it is acknowledged that there is a serious dislocation in human affairs, and in the human spirit. Nowhere is this more manifest than in the contemporary dilemma of peoples longing for peace yet armed to the teeth with weapons of mutual annihilation.

The Christian story of man's deliverance starts out from a radical diagnosis of this situation. The salvation it proclaims is a salvation from sin. No other word can be used to express what is meant, for " sin " is the Biblical word to signify man's plight, and no synonym can be found to convey its full meaning. By sin Christians mean our state of alienation from God and from one another, a fundamental dislocation in the relationship that we are meant to have as sons of the Father and brethren to one another. We have to distinguish *sins*—anger, greed, pride, and the like—from *sin* which is the state that produces them. The Christian Gospel announces a deliverance from sin which carries with it a promise of power for the overcoming of sins. We shall not understand the nature of this deliverance unless we realize something of the radical nature of sin as a description of our human existence.

The disclosure of God carries with it the picture of a family of men and women living in a mutually enriching harmony because they are all in fundamental harmony with God. The simplest illustration of what sin does to this relationship is that of a symphony orchestra in which each instrumentalist takes his eye off the conductor and begins to perform on his own. In other words, the root of the trouble is not in the social maladjustments of mankind but in their disobedience to God. This is throughout the Bible view of the matter. It could hardly be put more forcibly than in the words attributed to King David, " Against thee, thee only, have I sinned ", when we remember that the sin in question involved the most revolting crime against a fellow man. The point of the Genesis story about the temptation of the serpent in the Garden is precisely this: man's predicament goes back to a fundamental revolt against God. " Yea, hath God said . . . ? " Instead of owning God as Lord, each one of us sets out to be his own lord. The result is discord, and, but for the grace of God, chaos.

Original Sin has been interpreted in many ways in Christian theology, some of which are unacceptable to many Christians today. But the expression can still be used to signify this radical dislocation in the human scene—" original " in the sense that it cannot be traced to any one historical event, but belongs to the entire human race wherever it is, or has been, found. " For all have sinned ", says St. Paul, " and come short of the glory of God." [1] Jew and Gentile; white man and black man; British, Americans, Russians, Chinese—you and I—are sinners. The sin is ours: we are responsible.

This is the Christian diagnosis. It is a realistic appreciation of the situation. It is not a philosophical attempt to explain the origin of evil. We may say that it implies the existence of a sinfulness, or a sinful being, beyond human nature, but such speculation merely pushes the question of origin one stage farther back. We are not concerned with finding the answer to a baffling question, but with an acceptance of a real situation preparatory to hearing the practical solution. It is worth while, however, pausing to consider how much more radical the doctrine of sin is than some of its modern counterparts.

The most formidable rivals to the Christian

[1] Romans iii. 23.

diagnosis of the world's ills are probably those that may be conveniently labelled the Freudian and the Marxian. The Freudian finds the root of the trouble in psychological maladjustment; the Marxian in economic exploitation. It would be absurd to try to dismiss such massive systems in a few lines; but if this is in any way a fair summary of their diagnoses, one fact stands out in clear contradiction to the Christian doctrine. In spite of the element of truth that Christians must acknowledge in these descriptions of human ills, they are based on what we believe to be the fallacy of a " sinless class ". If all our ills are due to psychological maladjustment there must be one group of people (the psychiatrists?) who are normal and can provide the remedies. If all our ills are due to economic exploitation there is one group—in Communist dogma quite explicitly the proletariat—who are free from taint. In Christian doctrine there is no group, or individual, who is regarded as sinless. The one immaculate is Christ: all else are sinners. It follows therefore that in the Christian view, however much may and should be done in the psychological, economic, social, and political fields for the betterment of mankind, no fundamental solution of our problem can be reached from within the human situation. Help must come from beyond.

Before we turn to the understanding of that help as it is offered in Christ, there is another alternative view of our situation that we should note: for it has perhaps a greater influence than either the Freudian or the Marxian. Many people today, in reaction from the over-confidence and optimism of the last generation, are prepared to throw up the sponge and deny all responsibility whatever for the state of the world or their own souls. Grasping at theories propounded by some geneticists and psychologists, they are disposed to accept the " mess we are in " and put the blame, if any, on our glands or our great-grandmothers. Needless to say, if we are prepared to avoid responsibility in this way we shall find no meaning in a Gospel of salvation. But we should equally in strict logic find no meaning in courts of justice, our everyday expressions of praise or blame—in short, in life itself. The Gospel can, of course, scarcely be understood in such a context. But it is not a point of view that can be consistently held by any who are really alive—alive enough, for instance, to read this book and believe that it matters whether they agree or disagree.

The Christian diagnosis of the human situation might seem to be one of pure pessimism were it not that it forms the basis of a message of positive hope. It is, in fact, not nearly so pessimistic as the prevalent attitude of irresponsible despair; and less pessimistic in its effects than the disillusionments of scientific humanism. For it simply acknowledges our total responsibility for human disharmony, and our inability to develop from within man's own resources the motive power of his salvation. But in doing so it reminds us of our stature in God's sight. To be totally independent creatures plunging forward in the history that Gibbon called " the register of the crimes, follies, and misfortunes of mankind " would indeed be a hopeless situation. But to be " fallen sons of God " implies at least the possibility of restoration and deliverance. In this sense it is better to be a fallen angel than an imperfectly-evolved animal. To say " I have sinned " is at least a confession that we are dependent beings, made for the communion with God which we have broken; and when we can say it with sincerity the way is open to hear the word of forgiveness.

The Christian message of man's deliverance is founded entirely on the action of God. If the root of human evil is to be found in our alienation from God, then only God can release us. This does not mean that Christians despise man's efforts at education, social progress, elimination of fear, want, war, and disease; but rather that they find the impetus for such activity in the prior discovery of God's action to restore us to him. Many human ills can be conquered by the determination and inventive genius of men, but no human effort whatever can restore us to God. The entire religious activity of mankind—and it is a major factor in the human story in every corner of the world—can be seen as an effort to build a bridge from the kingdom of sin to the kingdom of God. Worship, prayer, sacrifice, incantation—in a thousand forms from the most primitive to the sublime—have been offered in the attempt to restore man to the Father. The Christian attitude to this world-wide religious tradition can be easily misunderstood. The Christian does not say: " These are all false tracks; come, and we'll show you *our* way to God." He says rather: " Whatever is true and genuine in all this religious activity is a response to God's approach to us. And in Christ we have found the bridge completed, not from our side but from God's."

The entire New Testament echoes with the conviction that in Christ a new era has dawned for the human race, and this new era is one in which God has opened the way to harmony with himself. It is variously described as " the Kingdom of God ",

" forgiveness of sins ", " victory over sin and death ", " everlasting life ", " redemption ", " salvation ", and other terms denoting the solution of the problem created by sin. No one could read these documents without having to acknowledge that the writers, each in his own way, are overpowered by the sense of a new and world-changing act of God. The writers of the Gospels report the announcement of Jesus that the Kingdom of God has come, and are filled with the joyful certainty that the promises of the Old Testament have come to fruition. The apostles are described in the Book of the Acts as telling the Jews that Jesus is their promised Messiah, and the Gentiles that the risen Christ has come to turn them from darkness to light. Paul's letters are inspired variations on the theme that " if any man is in Christ he is a new creature ". The Johannine writings are dominated by the master-thought that " the darkness is past, and the true light now shineth ". And the Book of the Revelation sets the Christian message in the dazzling imagery of " a new heaven and a new earth ".

This theme is taken up by the Church in a chorus of proclamation, prayer, and song. " Thou art the King of glory, O Christ: thou art the everlasting Son of the Father; When thou tookest upon thee to deliver man thou didst not abhor the Virgin's womb." Christ is celebrated in his Church as the Liberator who ushers in the Kingdom of God. In the early days the contrast between life in Christ and life in the kingdom of sin was acutely felt, and the water of baptism marked the distinction before all eyes. In later days the growth of Christendom has partly obscured this emphasis, but still the Church rests on the deliverance wrought by its Lord and celebrates it continually in word and sacrament. And in the deep experience of the believer the conviction holds that Christ has done for him what no one else could do, and that to know him is life eternal.

But what is it that Christ has done? How has he effected a deliverance, a change in our human status before God, and given us an immortal hope? The answer to this question contains the heart of the Gospel—the good news that is the central content of the Christian Faith.

" God ", says St. Paul, " was in Christ, reconciling the world unto himself." [1] This reconciliation took place in a way that passes ordinary understanding, and yet can dawn as God's satisfying truth on a receptive, childlike spirit. From the beginning it was " a stumbling-block to the Jews ", who expected another kind of deliverer, and " foolishness to the Greeks ", who could not fit a crucifixion and a resurrection into their philosophy. Yet it is profoundly based on the realities of our situation as lost sons of God. A lost son can be won home neither by brute force nor clever argument, but by one means only. And that means is love.

Man's deliverance, according to the Christian Faith, depends utterly on the love of God in action. This love in action, which reaches down to the lost where they are and offers them a forgiveness which they cannot earn, is known in the Bible as " grace ". The Old Testament, which seems at times to speak as if man could win his way to God by keeping the law, is in fact dominated by this thought of grace. In it we read of God's continuous initiative for the rescue of mankind. The people of God (that is

[1] II Corinthians v. 19.

what " Israel " means) ; the law of God ; the
prophets and the priests, are all aspects of the covenant that God makes with his rebellious people.   The
peculiar history of the Jews is recounted not because
they were a people of specific " religious genius "
but because God was acting through them for the
deliverance of the whole world.   When we reach the
New Testament every hint and promise of this grace
is abundantly fulfilled.   Christ stands among men
as the living embodiment of the loving action of God.
He makes no demand on them save that of trust and
love.   He comes to call not those who claim to be
righteous but " sinners " to repentance.   And in
him men and women who could make no claim whatever upon God found pardon and new life.

The clue to what God has done in Christ by his
grace is to be found in two small recurring words of
the New Testament: " for us ".   In Jesus Christ
God identified himself with the human race.   Instead of overcoming the evil situation by a word of
authority,   which   would   have   destroyed   our
humanity, he came to meet it " for us ".   Thus
Christ was born into a humble family and involved
from the beginning in a complicated and dangerous
social and political situation.   When he began his
public ministry he made himself one with contemporary sinners by submitting to baptism at the
hands of John.   As he passed through the towns and
villages of Palestine he continually sought out the
most needy in body and spirit.   He was deliberately
identifying himself with sin in all its guises—not as
a sinner himself, but " for us ".   As we read the
narrative we can see how towards the climax he
drew on himself the fire of the enemy.   Instead of
avoiding the issue he " set his face to go to Jeru-

salem ", where he knew that the concentrated hatred of his enemies awaited him. The temptations that he had already experienced " for us " were repeated as the Cross loomed nearer. Yet he went on to die " for us ".

The Crucifixion, which is described in some detail in the Gospels, does not read like a martyrdom. And there is no attempt whatever to arouse mere sympathy or sentiment on behalf of the victim. It is spoken of rather as a battle deliberately undertaken " for us ", a final and once-for-all engagement between God and sin, in which Jesus Christ, on our behalf, allows the forces of evil to do their worst. Everything we recognize as the symptoms of sin is there—hatred, cruelty, greed, fear, indifference, treachery. And everything we know to be God's is there—the triumphant love that prays for the enemy. " It is finished," he cries. And it looked as if God's cause was finished. Here was absolute goodness meeting concentrated evil, and death claimed the Son of God.

He died for our sins. The Christian Faith sees in this death not a martyrdom but a sacrifice. The Son of Man is offering for man what he cannot offer for himself—a perfect life. This is what is meant by " the blood of Christ "—the blood means the life poured out. The whole story of sacrifice in man's struggle to win his way to God finds its meaning here. God provides the sacrifice. And man is redeemed by the blood of Christ. If we find this difficult to understand we must remember that there are many ways of trying to explain how Christ died " for us ", and none have ever exhausted the mystery. Yet, in one way or another, Christians have always known that Christ went to his cross instead of them, winning a battle that they could not win.

But where was the victory? In the Resurrection of Christ from the dead. The Cross is not the Gospel without the Resurrection. This is the one supreme fact of history on which the Christian Faith depends. The Christ who was crucified was raised from the dead. If you were to remove that fact from the New Testament books there would be little left. If it were not for that fact, indeed, they would never have been written. For the first Christians literally staked their lives on the truth of the Resurrection. The apostles derived their authority in the Church from the fact that they were eye-witnesses of the risen Christ. St. Paul was not himself a witness of the actual Resurrection, but he claimed that his meeting with the risen Lord on the Damascus road was a privileged experience of the Resurrection when " it pleased God to reveal his Son in me ". His testimony, the earliest that is available to us in written form, to what was believed among contemporary Christians is of primary importance. " I delivered unto you ",[1] he says to the Corinthian Church, referring to an earlier visit, " first of all that which I also received, how that Christ died for our sins according to the Scriptures; and that he was buried, and that he rose again the third day according to the Scriptures: and that he was seen of Cephas, then of the twelve: after that, he was seen of above five hundred brethren at once; of whom the greater part remain unto this present, but some are fallen asleep." Whatever the modern world may make of the Resurrection as a subject for historical, psychological, or scientific investigation (and most

[1] I Corinthians xv. 3–6.

authorities would have a more open mind on the subject than their predecessors), it is quite certain that the first Christians were persuaded that the Jesus who had been crucified had risen from the dead, had been seen alive again by many of his followers, and was still alive in the world.

The death and Resurrection of Christ are sometimes described by Christians as " saving acts of God ". This kind of language is not very easy for a generation that is accustomed to separate acts and ideas. We recognize what are called historical facts: and we recognize religious ideas. What we find difficult is to connect the two. Thus, " Jesus was crucified and rose again " makes sense as an historical statement, whether we assent to it or not; and " God can deliver us from sin " makes sense as a religious proposition, whether or not we have experienced such deliverance. But the meaning of a " saving act " lies precisely in the bringing together of the historical statement and the religious proposition. The Christian belief is that through the death and Resurrection of Jesus Christ God delivers us from sin. The act and the salvation go together, and can never be separated without falsifying Christian truth. The Resurrection, for instance, is not simply a statement that about two thousand years ago a man in Palestine who had been killed was seen alive again. That would be remarkable, but possibly not unique, and could provoke the vulgar but expressive " So what? " Nor is the Resurrection simply a statement that God can raise mankind from sin and death. That would be a religious proposition without specific content—attachable, as it were, to any set of facts we choose. The " saving fact " of the Resurrection is that Christ rose " for us ". " He rose " is the historical fact; " for us " carries its significance.

When we think soberly about historical events we shall find that this combination of " fact " and " significance " is not peculiar to Christianity, but embedded in all our judgments on past events. The Battle of Britain was not simply an event. It was event plus significance. In a real sense we could say that it was a " saving fact ". Not all events have this kind of significance, so that it should not be an insuperable difficulty for us that certain specific historical events should have a supreme significance for us in the disclosure of God and the deliverance of man. Biblical history is always history of this kind. The facts are there, because this is a record of things that happened; but these particular facts are recorded because of the significance they have in the relationship of man to God.

The Christian Faith here makes this uncompromising assertion—that in a certain part of the world, at a definite point in time, God acted in human history in a decisive way to deliver mankind. In the life, death, and Resurrection of Jesus Christ the struggle between good and evil reached its climax, the love of God met and conquered the power of sin and death. The apostles tell us through the New Testament records: " This is what happened—and this is what it means." Jesus was born: that is the fact. " When the fulness of the time was come, God sent forth his Son . . ." [1]—that is the meaning. Jesus taught and preached and healed: that is the fact. " I am come that they might have life, and that they might have it more abundantly " [2]—that is the meaning. Jesus was crucified: that is the

[1] Galatians iv. 4.   [2] St. John x. 10.

fact. " God commendeth his love toward us, in that, while we were yet sinners, Christ died for us " [1] —that is the meaning. Jesus rose from the dead: that is the fact. " Thanks be to God which giveth us the victory through our Lord Jesus Christ " [2]— that is the meaning.

The work of Jesus Christ for the deliverance of man can be described by the use of many different kinds of symbols, images, and metaphors. The Bible itself provides a wide variety of ways of understanding the conquest of sin and death. We read of atonement—the work of Christ in making man at-one with God. We read of redemption, with its suggestion of deliverance from a state of slavery—at a cost. We read of salvation, the saving of mankind from the power and penalties of sin. We read of sacrifice—the offering brought by man to God. We read of the light that shines in the darkness, the defeat of the powers of evil, the ransom given, the debt forgiven, the peace bestowed, the cleansing effected, the regeneration of mankind. We read of man's justification, whereby he is set in a right relationship to God, and of the mediation that Christ makes between God and man. In all these, and many other, ways the Bible speaks to us of Christ's deliverance, the work that he came to do. Sometimes a group of Christians will fasten on one of these pictures, or ways of explanation, and make it the exclusive test of orthodox belief. Sometimes another group of Christians will reject one of these pictures as unacceptable to " the modern mind ". Yet all these Biblical images are aspects of the one great truth—that Christ lived, died, and rose again " for us ", to reconcile us to God.

[1] Romans v. 8.   [2] I Corinthians xv. 57.

This deliverance and reconciliation has its origin, its movement, and its end, entirely in the love of God. " Herein is love, not that we loved God, but that he loved us, and sent his Son to be the propitiation [yet another figure] for our sins." [1] We might put it this way: God could not forcibly reconcile us to himself, since he wants us to be sons not robots: God could not ignore the sin which is an open rebellion against his holiness: God could not leave us to perish, since that would be to fail in his creative purpose. So God did the unimaginable, yet the only thing: he sent his Son, his other Self, to join man in the depth—the last and bitterest depth, where sin cuts us off from the holy God and death claims the victory—so that for us, with us, and in us, he might conquer. This was the way of love. The Jews awaited a Messiah to deliver them. Jesus came as the Messiah they could not understand— the King who would use no instrument but love. The Temptations show how he rejected all other methods—materialist, spectacular, titanic—and chose to be the Suffering Servant of Isaiah's prophecy, who " was wounded for our transgressions . . . and with whose stripes we are healed ".[2]

Since love was the method of deliverance there could be no automatic response. This is the answer to the inevitable question: Why, if the decisive victory has been won, are we still engaged in the struggle with evil? The climax is indeed behind us, as in the last great war by the end of 1942 the Battles of El Alamein and Stalingrad had already decided the issue; but, as then there lay ahead still years of struggle to reach final victory, so in human history the decisive battle of Calvary is followed by

[1] I John iv. 10.   [2] Isaiah liii. 5.

continuous engagement until the final victory is made clear.   And in this period—represented in the Bible as that between Christ's first coming and his coming in final judgment—the deliverance wrought by Christ has to be accepted in faith in response to his love.   " The grace of our Lord Jesus Christ " is the victorious power of Christ alive in the world, but still remains grace, not force.   Therefore the key to the Christian deliverance is not " by power are ye saved willy-nilly ", but " by grace are ye saved through faith ".   We can see how this links up with the Christian conception of God as Father.   Experience teaches us that a son who goes wrong cannot be saved by force, but only by the kind of love that can elicit trust and hope.   And this response can never be guaranteed.   So it is with our relationship to God.   What he has done for us in Christ is entirely adequate for our deliverance and restoration, but it is an approach that awaits a response. The Gospel remains an invitation.   The Christ who has died for our sins and risen in victory is still the King who reigns incognito, and patiently awaits recognition.   His followers may sometimes be impatient with the world, as were the disciples when a village of the Samaritans " did not receive him ". " Lord, wilt thou that we command fire to come down from heaven, and consume them, even as Elias did?   But he turned, and rebuked them, and said, Ye know not what manner of spirit ye are of." [1] If we are to know, as Christians, what manner of spirit we are of, we must renounce all methods of force in the conversion of the world and depend on the simple and majestic invitation of Christ : " Come unto me."

St. Luke i x. 54–55.

The Christian symbol of deliverance is a cross. It
is familiar to us a hundred ways—in churches, on
badges, in hymns, on memorials, on flags, woven
into the fabric of Christendom and inescapable.
The legend associated with the cross—" In this sign
conquer "—is misinterpreted wherever and whenever it becomes the slogan of power-evangelism,
whether the power be military, political, or psychological. For the sign of the Cross reminds us that
when God almighty acted to save the world he came
as a little child, who grew up in a humble home, and
gave himself utterly into the hands of sinful men.
The deliverance was effected through suffering
freely endured and victoriously transformed. God's
way of deliverance was the way of good out of evil—
the greatest good out of the greatest evil. This is
why in the Christian Faith the salvation of the world
is bound up with what happened once " under
Pontius Pilate ".

It is necessary to add that this deliverance won by
Christ is not to be understood as excluding from its
benefits those who either lived before the Christian
era or have been out of earshot of the Gospel. When
the early Christians said " There is none other name
under heaven given among men, whereby we must
be saved ",[1] they were stating the uncompromising
claim of the Church. There *is*, for us, no other
name. We cannot associate this deliverance with
any other but Christ. His sacrifice is perfect; his
offering complete. But this does not mean that God
changed his mind when Christ came, or that he is a
different God to those who have never heard of
Christ. The Son of God from all eternity represents the saving grace that is offered to man. And

[1] Acts iv. 12.

wherever there is an attitude of faith and sincerity toward God this same grace is operative. " In every nation he that feareth him, and worketh righteousness, is accepted with him "[1]—the speaker is the same Peter whose words have just been quoted. Yet for us these must be largely theoretical questions. We live A.D. And a " year of the Lord " means a year in the era of the grace offered through Christ's conquest of sin. Therefore the Christian Faith contains at its heart the proclamation that the world is redeemed in Christ and summons men everywhere to " repent and believe ".

For further reading:

" God was in Christ ": D. M. Baillie.

" The Work of Christ ": P. T. Forsyth.

[1] Acts x. 35.

CHAPTER V

THE LIFE OF THE SPIRIT

In all that has been said so far about the Christian Faith there has been a suggestion that our thinking about God, Christ, the Bible, the Church, and man himself can be merely theoretical. We can hold views about God—orthodox according to Christian standards—and yet have no real knowledge of him. We can have an understanding of the revelation and the salvation that come in Christ without either being real to us. We can take part in the work and worship of the Church and not truly belong to it. We can read the words of the Bible without hearing the Word of God. We can isolate ourselves from others and from God by " objectifying ", which means standing over against them in cool detachment as if we were ourselves the centre of all things.

We are more inclined to do this in the Western world since the Renaissance because, until recently, a view of man was current that encouraged us to regard ourselves as isolated units equipped with an adequate instrument for examining the world around us. On this view the individual man is the criterion by which all things are judged. He is the king of his castle and looks out over the battlements on a varied world containing inanimate objects, animals, men, and women—and, perhaps, God. Therefore he can feel somewhat detached from the world outside, and it may from time to time even appear unreal. In recent years all the sciences, as well as philosophy, have combined to destroy this picture of the isolated individual. We now know ourselves to be closely linked one to another, continually confronted by other " I's " challenging our point of view. And we are shown in the new picture of the universe how impossible it is to separate an " objective " world from the one who is observing it. The way is surely now clearer for us to understand the Christian Faith, not as a system of ideas explaining the world and God conceived as " out there ", but as the expression of a claim that is being made on us here and now.

This is just another way of saying that the Christian Faith has to do with the existential question " What shall I do ? " rather than with speculative ideas about the universe. This seems to be one of the points at which the Christian Faith becomes most opaque to many of our contemporaries. They are accustomed to receiving ideas about the world outside and are perfectly prepared to listen to, and even to accept, religious ideas if they seem to be reasonably coherent. But, as they often say, they don't *mean* anything. That is to say, they are not operative factors in daily living. Life would be pretty much the same even if tomorrow they were proved to be completely without foundation. If, however, the Christian Faith is really concerned with the practical question " What shall I do ? " then it must affect our daily existence as men and women. When we hear the Faith in these terms then it springs to life.

The one item of the Christian creed that has specifically to do with this existential, life-giving element in our religious beliefs is the Holy Spirit. Yet by a strange twist of theological history this is the doctrine above all others that seems to be associated with woolliness, unreality, and vague religiosity. Nearly every clergyman wrestles yearly at Whitsuntide with what seems a remote and shadowy subject —God the Holy Spirit. This may in our tongue be partly due to the unfortunate associations of the word " Ghost ", which was the Elizabethan equivalent of " Spirit ", but it is also due to the fact that God the Father conveys an image to our minds, and so does Jesus Christ, whereas the Holy Spirit suggests nothing more than some kind of religious influence.

An examination of the New Testament reveals that for the first Christians almost the precise opposite was true. Jesus Christ they had known, at first or second hand—but they were still puzzled as to how to express the mystery of his person. God the Father was surrounded by a dazzling mystery, " dwelling in light which no man can approach unto ". But the Holy Spirit was a present and living experience. This was God alive among them and within them. And by his Spirit everything else came alive—the Scriptures, the Church, themselves. The experience described in the Book of the Acts which took place on the day of Pentecost after the Crucifixion is the key to this Christian belief. What happened then cannot be put into the sober words of factual description, and so we find the poetic images of wind and fire and tongues. But the fact stands out vividly for all to read. These dispirited men and women, for whom the events of the Crucifixion and Resurrection seemed to have come and gone like a lightning flash that lit up everything for a brief moment and then died into night, were suddenly aware that God was among them, that Christ was still alive, and that what he had done was now and for ever operative among men. They became aware of themselves—not just as men made new, but as a company, a body, in whom the Spirit of God now lived. And it is remarkable that the chapter which describes this event, beginning with a " sound from heaven ",[1] ends with the economic experiment of communal living. This was not a new set of ideas. It was life.

The doctrine of the Holy Spirit, so far from being a kind of obscure addendum to the Christian creed, is the expression of that which gives life to the whole. To know what it means is to be delivered from the realm of religious theory, from the ivory castle whence we survey the world and God, and to be confronted with the living God himself. It is also to be delivered from misleading views about the nature of the Christian life. When the Nicene Creed says " I believe in the Holy Ghost, the Lord and Giver of life " the reference is to this animating power by which doctrine is transmuted into action. The Holy Spirit means God becoming living and real to us; Christ being recognized within us; the Bible becoming the Word of God to us; the Church being the Body of Christ of which we are living members; and you and I finding our true selves in the " fellowship of the Spirit ". The Holy Spirit is the means of entrance into the world of Christian freedom and spontaneous obedience which in the New Testament is so clearly contrasted with the world of religious legalism and slavish conformity to a code.

When we come to consider the doctrine of the Trinity we can better understand why this aspect of God's relationship to us should be expressed in

[1] Acts ii. 2.

terms of a third Person in the Godhead. Meanwhile it is important to see that the doctrine of the Spirit tells us something vital about the Christian God. It is worth noting the kind of words that are associated in the New Testament with the Holy Spirit. They are words like " life ", " love ", " liberty ", " power ", " unity ", " fellowship "—all having reference to the practical effects of the presence of God in our human life. In general, we may say that the Holy Spirit in the Bible stands for " God in action ". To believe in the Spirit means therefore that God for us can never be a mere idea, or a distant Deity without interest in his world, or an inscrutable Lawgiver who exacts his rewards and penalties. God the Holy Spirit is God alive and free, God here and now present to his people, God completely able to manipulate his creation. It is by God's Spirit that we are maintained in life from moment to moment. It is by God's Spirit that we find the new life in Christ. It is by God's Spirit that we are guided forward in the Christian life and led into new reaches of truth and love.

Dr. Julian Huxley has spoken of God as " an unnecessary hypothesis " in modern thought. In so far as he was referring to certain theories about God that have been commonly held, he was probably right. To believe in a God who is merely a stop-gap—one who is accepted as an easy way of supplying the gaps in our scientific knowledge—is not much more than a form of superstition. It is not surprising that when such belief cracks under the successive advances of science towards the closing of the gaps it is seen to be an " unnecessary hypothesis ". It always was. The result, however, of the discarding of inadequate conceptions of God without replacing them with a knowledge of the living God is to leave what Dr. Huxley calls a " God-shaped blank " in the modern consciousness. This blank can never be filled with humanistic theories or scientific idealism. Nor can it be filled with a still more cunningly contrived stop-gap God. It can only be filled, as it always has been in human experience, by a direct confrontation with the living God—the God in action who is the Holy Spirit. We have an incurable tendency to think of God in the past tense: he is the one who made the world, the God of Abraham, of the prophets and apostles; he is the God in whom our fathers believed when they tried to understand the world in which they lived. We are slow to believe in a God who is as active now as in the days of Moses. But the " God-shaped blank " will not be filled by the God of Moses, but only by a God who is alive and in action *now*. It is of such a God that we speak when we say: I believe in the Holy Ghost. The Holy Spirit is God contemporary.

What we are now considering is the realization of the Christian facts in terms of action here and now. We have seen that the Christian deliverance arises out of the action of God in Christ " under Pontius Pilate ". Christ died for our sins and rose again for our justification, as we read in the New Testament. But what we want to know is how we can be delivered in this present age. In what way does the work of Christ two thousand years ago affect my life and action today?

There are two ways in which we are linked with the events of first-century Palestine, two ways in which we can understand how what happened then and there can be effective for us here and now. One

D

is the way of continuous tradition. There exists a society of men and women stretching over the centuries and through the nations preserving in more than one way an unbroken link with the apostolic age: the Church. When we come to that item in the creed (for belief in the Church is part of the Christian Faith) we shall see how this continuous society is more than an organization for associating Christian believers and canalizing their faith. Meantime it is clear that here is one method by which the original Christian facts can be communicated to us in the twentieth century. But it is with another means that we are now concerned.

The other method by which these distant events can be actualized is by the direct action of God upon us—individually and as a community. We all know what is commonly meant by " realizing " an experience. We read every day in the newspapers of accidents, murders, and other tragic events. Then one day, perhaps, we find ourselves personally involved in such a tragedy. " I never realized until now . . ." is our instinctive response. Until then such events were read of, understood, believed: we may even have known a passing sympathy. But when the event touches *us*—that is different: that is realization. The same thing can happen with a past event of which we have known. There comes a day with most men and women when they realize, in some measure, what has been done for them by their fathers and mothers. It may be one particular event of which they have known for years that suddenly comes alive for them, and they say: " Now I realize what was done for me." It is this kind of realization that happens to us when the events of Calvary and Easter morning are suddenly no longer mere historical happenings and become in a mysterious way *ours*. This is the work of God the Holy Spirit.

An eighteenth-century nobleman in Germany looking one day at a painting of the Crucifixion found that this was no longer a familiar representation of a distant event. The eyes of the Crucified seemed to look right at him and say: " All this I have done for thee; what hast thou done for me? " This experience of Zinzendorf, the founder of the Moravian brotherhood, is by no means unusual in Christian history up to the present time. But such realization need not be sudden and dramatic. For millions it has come quietly and unobserved; yet it has happened. They could say, " Once I was blind: now I can see ", without being able to put any date to the awakening. In every case what happens is that the work of Christ *for us* becomes the work of Christ *in us*. Unless this could happen, the Christian Faith would be merely a set of beliefs about God and his way of salvation without any significance for our lives. To believe in the Holy Spirit is to believe in God " in us ", actualizing and realizing what has been done " for us " through Christ.

We can see this happening in the records of the New Testament. For there we have the description of how men and women for whom the life, death, and Resurrection of Jesus Christ had already passed into history found themselves so united to him that they could speak of Christ and his work as contemporary. St. Paul puts it with characteristic vigour when he writes: " I am crucified with Christ: nevertheless I live; yet not I, but Christ liveth in me: and the life which I now live in the flesh I live by the faith of the Son of God, who loved me, and gave himself for me." [1]   This is not an extreme mysticism, the possession of an exalted spirit: it is the paradoxical expression of the everyday life of a Christian in any age.   The saving acts of Christ become our acts; he lives in us; by the Holy Spirit we *realize* the events of Christ's life, death, and resurrection.   All the letters of the New Testament, which are our authority for the beliefs of the first Christians, are saturated with this conviction that the work of Christ can become contemporary, that he who died for us can live in us, and that the Christian life consists in the realization through the Spirit of these saving facts.   The First Epistle of John, speaking a very different language from Paul's, is a witness to the same experience.   " And this is his commandment, That we should believe on the name of his Son Jesus Christ, and love one another, as he gave us commandment.   And he that keepeth his commandments dwelleth in him, and he in him. And hereby we know that he abideth in us, by the Spirit which he hath given us." [2]   The author of the letter to the Hebrews speaks of " Jesus Christ, the same yesterday, and today, and for ever ", and prays " the God of peace, that brought again from the dead our Lord Jesus, that great shepherd of the sheep, through the blood of the everlasting covenant, make you perfect in every good work to do his will, working in you that which is well-pleasing in his sight, through Jesus Christ ". [3]

The experience of the day of Pentecost as recorded in the Book of the Acts is the origin and pattern of this realization of the Christian facts.   The situation is normative for all that has followed.   Here

---

[1] Galatians ii. 20.   [2] I John iii. 23–24.   [3] Hebrews xiii. 20–21.

were men and women who had actually seen the
" saving facts ". They had known Jesus, had
watched him die, had seen him alive again. But, as
we have already noted, these facts were still con-
fusing; and were rapidly becoming remote. They
had not been realized. When the Spirit came the
situation entirely changed. You could say that
while before they had believed in the Resurrection,
now they knew that the Spirit of Christ was alive in
them. The preaching of Peter that day, and the
subsequent sermons recorded in the Book of the Acts,
show how a recital of the saving facts could become a
decisive challenge to all who heard. This is, on the
face of it, quite extraordinary. Why should the
announcement that Jesus had died and risen again
lead to a change in the lives of ordinary men and
women—or to violent passions of fear and rage?
Yet this happened in every place where these facts
were preached. The only kind of explanation
offered is something like " the Holy Ghost came upon
them ". That is to say that God the Spirit
actualized these facts for them and in them. They
were no longer deeds done beyond and apart from
them, but deeds they could realize.

This throws light on what the Christian means
when he says " I believe ". Such a statement means
much more than an assent to certain religious propositions. It indicates a degree of personal commitment by which certain historical facts are
accepted and absorbed. The original Greek of the
Creed could be translated " I believe into ", suggesting this note of identification with what is professed. We believe *in* certain historical facts, but we
believe *into* the people who embody them. We can
believe in the fact that " on the third day he rose

again from the dead "; but it is another thing to believe into the living Christ.

The Christian Faith thus means much more than a series of propositions about God, supported by historical statements about Jesus Christ. The moment we say " I believe in the Holy Ghost " we are expressing the personal, contemporary, actual significance of it all to us. God is no longer an idea, even an orthodox idea: he is the living God in action, evoking the question " What shall I do? " rather than " How shall I think? " And the facts about Jesus Christ become charged with meaning for us. This is the reason why the creeds seem to say so little about important matters of faith and action. Belief in the Holy Ghost carries with it the entire meaning of the Christian life. For that life is " life in the Spirit ".

It would be artificial to delay all discussion on the sacraments until a later chapter. Their significance cannot be avoided at this point. For they are the sign and the means of this life-giving union with Jesus Christ, this actualizing of the saving facts. To be baptized means to be united with him in his death and Resurrection. This is the plain meaning of St. Paul's statement: " Therefore we are buried with him by baptism into death: that like as Christ was raised up from the dead by the glory of the Father, even so we also should walk in newness of life." [1] Such teaching may not be readily understood, and is open to many kinds of interpretation, but the fact that in baptism we are made to share in Christ's work and to receive its benefits is clear not only here but in other references in the New Testament. Baptism is the sacrament of Christian initiation, and

[1] Romans vi. 4.

is spoken of in the Book of the Acts in connection with repentance and the gift of the Holy Spirit. It both signifies and conveys " the Spirit of life " by which we enter into a realization of what God has done for us in Christ. Similarly, the sacrament of the Lord's Supper is the most powerful sign and seal of our continued union with Christ. Again we may not fully understand just how Christ comes to us in the bread and the wine, but it is perfectly clear that the New Testament teaches throughout that by this means we are united with him, and realize in ourselves what he has done for us. In both sacraments the Church invokes the Holy Spirit, the " Lord and Giver of life ", by whose action Christ and his saving work are made contemporary for us and in us.

This " Spirit of life " is not only the clue to the linking of past events with present experience through union with Christ. The same train of thought will lead us to an understanding of the nature of the Christian life. That life cannot, as is popularly supposed, be conceived in isolation from Christian belief. The two are inseparably linked. As we believe—really believe, in the sense we have been considering—so we act. Conversely, by our actions we reveal what we truly believe. To say that we believe in the Holy Spirit should carry with it a commitment to a certain kind of life, just as a certain kind of life will reveal, however we might express it, that we believe in the Holy Spirit. How, then, are we to describe the nature of the Christian life?

The Christian life begins and continues as a relationship between us and God. Through Christ the Son we are called to become sons and daughters of God, and our life finds its meaning and its motives

within that family relationship. Thus the entire
Christian ethic is summed up in one word: love.
To the question " What shall I do? " Jesus replied by
eliciting the summary of the Jewish Law: " Thou
shalt love the Lord thy God with all thy heart, and
with all thy soul, and with all thy strength, and with
all thy mind; and thy neighbour as thyself." [1]
Love to God as our Father and to men as our
brethren is the all-embracing principle. There are
no others that are absolute. We must notice, however, that this " law " is already contained in
Judaism; and other religions are not without similar
indications of man's chief duty. What is there that
is distinctive and unique in the Christian way of
life?

First, we can see from the New Testament that
love is made the central and controlling factor for
our entire understanding of the life to which God
calls us in Christ. Love may enter into the teaching
of other religions, may even be given the first place,
as in the Old Testament passage acknowledged and
accepted by Jesus. But for Christianity love is the
entire meaning and content of the Christian life,
because it is the very nature of the family-relation-
ship we have with God in Christ. God *is* love.
So central was this thought to the first Christians
that they found most of the words that were in
common use inadequate to express what they knew
to be a new power released into the world. " Eros "
was the Greek word in popular language which was
used to denote a kind of love that was nearer to the
Hollywood than the holy. " Philia " was used of
the affection of friends; " philadelphia " of love in a
family; " philanthropia " to describe a humane and

---

[1] St. Luke x. 27.

courteous attitude. None of these seemed adequate to indicate the utter self-giving of Christ and the kind of universal indiscriminate care for others that he inspired in his followers. So they took a relatively neutral word " Agapé " and used it consistently to describe this new power that the Holy Spirit had made known among men. The world in part understood that this was a unique phenomenon and " Agapé " became the recognized expression covering the Christian conception of God's love to man, man's love to God, and man's love to his fellows. It was inclusive and absolute : no higher law could be recognized. Thus Jesus could say to his followers : " A *new* commandment I give unto you, That ye love one another ; as I have loved you, that ye also love one another." [1]

Again, the Christian Faith takes very seriously the question of our ability to love God, and to care for our fellows in the disinterested way that the commandment implies. If you talk with a Muslim you will probably find that he regards this way of life as a sheer impossibility, and an unpractical proposal. If, however, you discuss the subject with the average vaguely-religious Western you will probably detect an underlying conviction that love to God is a natural attitude and that love for our fellows, while difficult, is the simple duty of the decent citizen. The New Testament view is neither the plain pessimism of the Muslim nor the optimism of the average Western. Jesus and his apostles are under no illusions that this love is a simple possibility for man. The power of self-love (going beyond its legitimate expression, which is assumed in the commandment to love our neighbours *as ourselves*), in the form of covetousness,

[1] St. John xiii. 34.

pride, anxiety, complacency, and the like, is flood-lighted in the pages of the New Testament. It is certainly not taken for granted that a man or woman can decide to adopt the rule of love and carry it out by an act of will. The Sermon on the Mount was not a set of moral maxims handed out to man-kind like an instruction booklet for a car. If we read it seriously and carefully we find we are con-fronted with the absolute demands of the life of love, demands which have been fulfilled by Jesus and by no one else. We find that this is a picture of life in his Kingdom, but we are left with the vital problem of how we get into this Kingdom. And that drives us back on the person and work of Christ himself. To experience the ways of the Kingdom we have first to accept the invitation of the King.

The Christian life thus begins with our confession. We are not those who love God and our fellows; we are astray from the Kingdom or the family of God. There is nothing in us that must claim or deserve his love. This confession and the desire to receive the Kingdom, to be restored to the family, is what the New Testament means by repentance. The effect of the Christian proclamation of the way of love must always be to drive us to repentance. This is the work of the Holy Spirit; for it means that God speaks directly to us in our present situation. We then no longer think of the commandment of love as being a natural ethical code to follow, but as a Word of God to us that drives us to seek forgiveness and new life. In this Christianity is radically different from all religious systems that rest upon a demand from God which we feel capable of meeting in our own strength. The insistence that we begin with repentance, the renunciation of any claims on

God based on our moral achievements, the stress on humility and the need to become " as little children " —these are essentials of the Christian Faith that have often been a cause of reproach. This is the " slave mentality " against which the nineteenth-century devotees of the super-man fulminated, echoed in our own day by Hitler, among others. This is the point of entrance that is in some measure repugnant to us all—the wicket-gate to which we must stoop. There is no more consistent teaching in the New Testament than upon this point. Christ and his apostles reiterated that to enter the Kingdom of love we must abandon all claims upon God and seek humbly to receive forgiveness and the Spirit of life.

" God be merciful to me a sinner." [1] This, according to Jesus, was the prayer that " justified ", not the claim of the Pharisee: " God, I thank thee I am not as other men are." The heart of the conflict with the scribes and Pharisees was this difference on the basic approach to God. We must remember that many of them represented the best among the religious traditions of the time. Yet the message of Jesus aroused the bitterest opposition among them. For it seemed that his practice of going to the lowest strata of society, his parables about God's limitless grace, his teaching that righteousness was not a matter of a slavish fulfilment of the law, were all desperately dangerous for the people. This was one of the main counts against him which led to his arrest: he was an innovator, a destroyer of religious tradition. The apostles in the early days of the Church encountered the same hostility. Wherever they brought the message of God's free forgiveness to

[1] St. Luke xviii. 10–14.

the penitent sinner they offended the religious and amused the cynical. But this they knew to be the core of the new message. We cannot begin to love in the Christian sense until the Spirit of God has led us to receive " as little children " the overwhelming love of Christ for us.

The temptation, however, to base our lives on our own achievements, to claim merit before God for our actions, is deeply rooted in our human nature. We tend to prefer a religion of law to a religion of love in our heart of hearts. For law-religion seems clear and definite and gives us the satisfaction of apparent attainment. To live by law means marking the score, with the consequent tendency to despair when we fail and self-righteousness when we succeed ; and it begets a hardness of heart in our judgment of others. Yet it is the way in which we most naturally consider our religious life, and no organized religion has ever completely eliminated its influence. Within a few years of the coming of the Spirit at Pentecost, St. Paul could write to a church that they " had fallen from grace " and lapsed into a new legalism. Within a few days even, we can trace the strength of the old legalism within the apostolic group struggling against this new vision of our relationship with God. To this day Christianity is continually being perverted into a law-religion. It happens in every section of the Church. Whenever rules and principles are exalted above love; whenever human merit is suggested as the basis for our acceptance with God ; whenever a hardness of heart settles upon the respectable and judgment of others' sins becomes dominant; whenever theological orthodoxy is exalted above the fruit of the Spirit—then we have fallen from grace into legalism.

We might summarize the life of the Spirit—the Christian life—in two words, indicating how it is contrasted with legalism on the one hand and licentiousness on the other. In all of us there is a tendency to oscillate between these two poles. It is because of the inner licentiousness of our hearts that we cling to a code of moral law. It is because we are irked by moral law that we swing towards licentiousness (in practice or in theory). The Christian life shows a way of escape from this dilemma by a response to the Spirit of God.

(1) The Christian life is marked by *liberty*. No one can miss the exhilarating note of freedom in the Gospels and Epistles. It is hard for those who have become accustomed to thinking of Christianity as a restraint and restriction upon human activities—a kind of moral policeman—to realize with what a sense of liberation the ancient world heard the Gospel. For the Jew it meant a liberation from the yoke of the law (in so far as it had become a mere burden to him). For the Gentile it meant a liberation from the fears of human and demonic powers. For both it meant a liberation from the control of sin and death. St. Paul could therefore speak of being delivered from the " bondage of corruption into the glorious liberty of the children of God ".[1] This is the characteristic of the new life in Christ.

When therefore we ask the question " What shall I do? " we must not expect a " Christian answer " in set terms. There is no code-book within the Christian Faith that can solve all our moral problems. We are given the freedom of sons. " Henceforth I call you not servants; for the servant knoweth

[1] Romans viii. 21.

not what his lord doeth: but I have called you friends." [1] What this means is surely that the Christian way of life depends on our free response to the Spirit of Christ. It is controlled by love, and by no other law. This was what St. Augustine meant when he said: "Love God, and do what you will." That could be a dangerous and immoral statement if we were to imagine that loving God meant having a vague sentimental feeling toward him on the basis of which we proceeded to obey every whim and impulse. What it really implies, of course, is that if we set ourselves steadily to love God in the power of his Spirit we shall find that our wills become his will—and therefore we can do what we like. The good that has been the goal of all sincere men and women in their moments of enlightenment is conceived in the Christian Faith not in terms of a set of rules to be observed, but as the fruit of a life " in the Spirit "—that is, in living response to Christ. Fruit is that which appears naturally, effortlessly, on a tree that is well planted and nourished. "The fruit of the Spirit ", says St. Paul, " is love, joy, peace, longsuffering, gentleness, goodness, faith, meekness, temperance: against such there is no law." [2] These qualities are not the result of our effort in keeping the law, constituting our claim upon God: they are the natural result of a life based on repentance and faith, grounded in Christ. In other words they are the by-product of the free relationship of a Son to a Father, and not the result of obeying copy-book maxims.

This freedom of the " life of the Spirit " also implies a spontaneity and extravagance that is contrary to all the instincts of legalism. You may

[1] St. John xv. 15.   [2] Galatians v. 22–23.

have noticed the number of times in the Gospels that we find Jesus commending the spontaneous gesture, the extravagant action. The parables are full of strange, and even shocking, behaviour: the stories are calculated to make us ask: " Why did this man, or this woman, act this way? " And when we see what is implied we find that we have another of the secrets of the Kingdom of God. Jesus welcomed such gestures as those of the men who broke up the roof to let their friend down into his presence, or of the woman who broke a valuable vase of ointment and poured it over his feet. For him the children of God ought never to be bound within the framework of the routine response, the copy-book behaviour, the moral ledger-book. That is why throughout the centuries the Christian Faith has been demonstrated by a vast variety of human types, each of them showing something of the infinitely variegated pattern of Christian love.

(2) It is equally important to realize that the life of the Spirit is a life of *obedience*. When Jesus issued his invitation, " Come unto me, all ye that labour and are heavy laden ",[1] the context shows that he had in mind particularly those who were labouring under the weight of a legalistic religion, and laden with the bad conscience which it inevitably induces. From this kind of duty-religion he offered rest, the peace and freedom that come with the new relationship of grace. But he added: " Take my yoke upon you, and learn of me." The freedom of the Christian life is not autonomy: it is freedom under the yoke of Christ.

The same train of thought appears in the passage where St. Paul made his famous diagnosis of the

[1] St. Matthew xi. 28.

failure of law-religion. " I delight in the law of God
after the inward man: but I see another law in my
members, warring against the law of my mind, and
bringing me into captivity to the law of sin. . . ." [1]
He describes the way in which a knowledge of the
law of God adds to the sense of guilt, and is impotent
to deliver. Then comes the answer: " The law of
the Spirit of life in Christ Jesus hath made me free
from the law of sin and death." But this freedom is
not just freedom *from* something: it is freedom *for*
something. It means being delivered from a
thraldom to an utterly new kind of service. We are
set free to obey God. " For as many as are led by the
Spirit of God, they are the sons of God." [2] That
is to say, to be a member of God's family in Christ,
is not simply to experience " the glorious liberty of
the sons of God ", but to be totally under the sway of
his Spirit.

This apparent paradox of the Christian life is
summarized by Jesus in a statement that occurs no
less than five times in the four Gospels. In St.
Luke's version it reads: "For whosoever will save his
life shall lose it: but whosoever will lose his life for
my sake, the same shall save it." [3] The Greek word
for " life " is here the same as that which is regularly
translated " soul ". We are being told that it is
only when we are willing to renounce the " I "
that we really discover ourselves; only when we
abdicate our sovereign rights that we discover our
real freedom. What we have all experienced in
some measure—noting how the more we try to assert
ourselves the less self there is to assert, and how when
we forget ourselves in others or in a good cause we
find our true selves—is here made the key to the

[1] Romans vii. 22–viii. 2.   [2] Romans viii. 14.   [3] St. Luke ix. 24.

Christian life. We only know the freedom of the life of the Spirit when we are prepared to abandon ourselves to the leading of the Spirit. The simple obedience of the Christian to what he learns of Christ in the Scriptures, the Church, and by his Spirit constitutes the " service that is perfect freedom ".

It is in this way, then, that Christian Faith and the Christian life are related. The Holy Spirit is God in action here and now, bringing us, through repentance and faith in Christ, into that status of sonship where we are free to obey the Father.

For further reading:

" A Man in Christ ": J. S. Stewart.
" The Way, the Truth, and the Life ": Macphail.

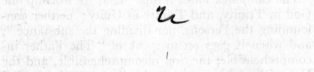

CHAPTER VI

THE TRINITY

WE are now in a position to consider a doctrine of the Christian Faith which is central in the teaching and worship of the Church, and yet appears to the average man to be hopelessly abstruse. The idea of the Trinity seems at first sight a typical piece of theological mystification. " In the unity of the Godhead ", says the Shorter Catechism, " there be three persons, of one substance, power, and eternity; God the Father, God the Son, and God the Holy Ghost." The Athanasian Creed makes an even more formidable assault on our understanding: " The Catholick Faith is this : That we worship one God in Trinity, and Trinity in Unity; neither confounding the Persons, nor dividing the substance ", and when it goes on to speak of " The Father incomprehensible, the Son incomprehensible, and the Holy Ghost incomprehensible " the modern mind has been tempted to add " and the whole thing incomprehensible ". This seems an unnecessarily complicated way of speaking about a God whom we claim to know as a living Being with whom we can have intelligible contact.

We have to remember that such credal definitions were not written as an introduction to the Christian Faith. They were drawn up by theologians whose job it is to express as carefully as possible the intellectual content of the Faith, excluding as far as humanly possible misleading or inadequate conceptions. They are standards of belief set up as guides to the thinking of the Church. It would be as sensible to confront an enquirer right away with the Athanasian definition of the Trinity, as to start a beginner in art with a treatise in æsthetics. We can only begin to appreciate what the creeds are expressing when we have already some practical experience of the Christian religion.

It does, however, strike the observer as odd that so much emphasis should be laid by the Church on the most puzzling item of its creed. There is no question about this emphasis. Not only is the Trinity expressed in creed and catechism, but it is a constantly-recurring note in Christian prayers, hymns, and blessings. We baptize " in the name of the Father, the Son, and the Holy Ghost "; we consecrate the elements of the Holy Communion, confirm, marry, dedicate in the same name; we sing " Glory be to the Father, and to the Son, and to the Holy Ghost "; we pray " God the Father, God the Son, and God the Holy Ghost, bless, preserve and keep you ". All the Churches that are members of the World Council, as well as the Roman Catholic Church, are avowedly and explicitly Trinitarian. The Unitarian Church, which rejects the doctrine (as its name implies), is isolated by this rejection more than if it were denying almost any other item of the Creed. It is clear that there must be some weighty reason for this tremendous emphasis— something more than the mere concern of theologians for the preservation of an intricate formula.

We find another clue to the importance of this doctrine in a curious feature of Church life and history. It seems to be generally true that the Christian community in every age has been nourished by a belief in the Trinity, so that when this belief has waned the strength of the Church has waned with it. Yet, on the face of it, some form of Unitarianism is a much simpler and more acceptable form of belief for the average man. To say that there is one God, and that Jesus was the best religious teacher, would seem so eminently reasonable that we might expect some such creed to attract millions to whom the Trinitarian formulæ had become obscure and unreal. This has never happened. On the contrary, Christian communities that abandoned the doctrine of the Trinity have nearly always tended to die away. Unitarian Churches have fostered some remarkable and distinguished figures, but they have seldom had any broad appeal to the masses in any country. Even today, when it may well be that a great many adherents of orthodox churches are actually Unitarian in their personal beliefs, there is no sign whatever of any major denomination moving in that direction.

Thus a casual inspection of the influence of the doctrine of the Trinity would suggest to a serious enquirer that there is much more here than theological mystification. And when we turn to the discovery of the origin and intention of the doctrine, we shall soon be on the track of its strange and exciting power.

Every part of the Christian Faith, as we have seen, has to do with God in action. We know Christ by what he does. We find God as he discloses himself. We are delivered by God's saving deeds for us, and his living Spirit in us. As this Gospel takes hold of us we find that, even before we have really thought much about it, we are already believers in the Holy Trinity. For we know that the Son who redeemed us is God " made flesh " for us: we know that the

Spirit who meets us now is God present to us: and we know that the Father who sends the Son and the Spirit is God almighty, maker of heaven and earth. Yet we know that these are not three Gods. Therefore when we come to set words to what has happened to us in our meeting with God can we find in the end any other way of speaking than to say that we believe in one God, who is Father, Son, and Holy Spirit?

It is important to realize that the doctrine of the Trinity did historically arise from this living experience of the Church. There was never any question of a group of theologians huddling together to work out a fascinating metaphysical exercise. Nor was there a formula waiting to be lifted from the pages of the Bible. Nor was it suddenly revealed to a council of the Church in a flash from heaven. What happened was much simpler and more natural. Men found themselves believing in the Trinity long before any formal definition was attempted. We know God by what he does; and, since they found that he had acted towards them as Father, Son, and Holy Spirit, One God, they found that when they wanted to speak of his being they could say no less. They were not bothered so much with logical tidiness, or popular simplicities: they desired to express the truth as the truth had been revealed to them in action. And this led them in the end to say: three persons and one God.

We can see the beginnings of this process in the pages of the New Testament. If the Bible were a handbook of theology we should expect to find the doctrine of the Trinity by at least the third chapter, explicitly stated as an article of Christian belief. But we are dealing with documents that come from life and not the study. In the New Testament the Gospels and the Book of the Acts tell us what happened: the Epistles tell us the meaning of what happened. And what *did* happen in this matter of men's knowledge of God's person? We find the disciples throughout firm believers in God the Father almighty, conscious of his actions in the history of their race and in their own lives. We then find them wrestling with the question of who this was who had come into their lives—this Messiah, this Christ, this Son of God. We find them at the various stages of understanding his relationship to God until they come to the full and final conviction that he and the Father are one. The Epistles develop this thought in terms of the Son of God existing in unity with the Father from eternity, and becoming man for our salvation. Then if we look again at the story of Pentecost we shall see that the disciples' conviction of the divine "aliveness" of Jesus with them was the work of the Holy Spirit. This Holy Spirit who revealed Christ to them could not himself be less than God. In the Epistles we read that "no man can say that Jesus is the Lord, but by the Holy Ghost".[1] So we find that the first Christians, when they spoke about God, sometimes spoke of the Father; sometimes of Jesus Christ; sometimes of the Holy Spirit. There is no constant order or pattern in their language: their experience led them quite naturally to think of the divine being in these three ways. Yet there could never for a moment be any suspicion that they believed in three Gods. When the suggestion is made that Trinitarianism is really a kind of disguised polytheism it is sufficient to recall that the first disciples were all Jews—and

[1] I Corinthians xii. 3.

for the Jew the first and most sacrosanct of all beliefs is in the unity of God. The word above all other words is : "Hear, O Israel: the Lord our God is one Lord." If the disciples had come from some other race it is conceivable that they might have thought in terms of three Gods: with Jews it was impossible. Therefore they proclaimed the one God—but spoke of him as by his actions they had to speak, as Father, Son, and Holy Spirit.

Thus it was within the context of the Church's life that the doctrine of the Trinity was first formulated. We could almost say that the first Christians lived in the Trinity before they applied their minds to the matter at all. And to this day the Trinity is for all Christians more meaningful in life and worship than in naked thought. It is none the less our right and duty to try to reason in this area of the Christian Faith. This is not only necessary in any attempt to explain what we believe to others. It is part of what is meant by the commandment to love God " with all our minds ".

It is, of course, easy to avoid all difficulties with religious doctrines by the simple process of saying, " It is a mystery." If nothing further can be said we are not really dealing so much with mystery as with mystification. But there is a real sense in which mystery is right and proper in any doctrine about God. An explanation of God's being which is crystal-clear must surely be suspect. If God is *God*, and not just a creation of our minds, how could he possibly be imprisoned in any intellectual formula of ours? Some popular expositions of the Christian Faith run into this danger. We want to have our God in a little parcel that can be handed out to all comers. And so we find ourselves speaking of him glibly and smoothly, referring to his nature as if it were simply human nature with the creases ironed out, and to his plans as if we were his chief-of-staff. Against all such platitudinizing of God the doctrine of the Trinity rears up a majestic barrier. There is that in God which defies all human thought and formulæ; there is mystery in his being that no theological telescope can penetrate; there is sovereignty in his actions that lies beyond our calculations. A god at the mercy of our intellects would, after all, be less than they. We could not worship a god who comes limping along in the wake of the human brain. Before the revelation of the One God in three Persons we can only bow in adoration and in awe.

Yet the Trinity is not *all* mystery. This is a way of conceiving of God that continually opens up new avenues of thought and life. We assume too easily that to say we believe in one God gives us a neater, clearer, and simpler answer than one that involves talking about three Persons in one God. Yet we know that truth is seldom to be expressed in one single satisfactory phrase. When we are dealing with what you might call the lower orders of truth a simple phrase may be perfectly adequate. Mathematical truth is of this kind, at least in its practical everyday expressions. When we reckon that eight half-crowns make a pound we feel that this is a truth which requires no qualification: it is perfectly satisfactory. When we are dealing with historical truth the matter becomes a little more complicated. " William the Conqueror landed in England in 1066 " may be a plain statement of fact, but it already suggests that there are all kinds of other considerations to be weighed before we can even approach the whole truth about this event. Was it " a good thing "? The answer to that famous question can hardly be given in a quick sentence. Then what is the truth about a work of art? or about an altruistic deed? or our experience of a sunset? In the higher regions of human life truth is seldom simple and easily expressed. Particularly is this so when we are speaking about people. Anyone who has to write testimonials for candidates seeking an appointment knows how extremely difficult it is to express the truth about anyone. If this is so with human beings how much more must it be so with the divine Being? If we think that we have made a sufficient and adequate statement when we say " God is one " it would be worth considering what that would mean when applied to someone we know. " Tom is one ", if it means anything, just tells us that there are not two separate people, but one Tom. Yet that is to say almost nothing. We supplement this truth continually, attributing all kinds of varied, and even contradictory, qualities to Tom. We even say, " There's more than one Tom ", referring to the baffling complexity of our human character. Why, then, in the highest order of existence of which we can conceive, should we think that we can express the truth in terms of naked unity?

We are obviously now in difficult territory, and must be wary of rushing in where philosophers fear to tread. But there is another aspect of this unity-problem that is relevant to our thought about God. Unity is clearly not the whole truth about man, not simply because he is a complex being, but more fundamentally because our personalities do not develop in isolation. We become persons in society— that is, by our contacts with other people. Society, if we can put it this way, is as essential an ingredient of human existence as unity. The importance of society, or community, is a re-discovery of our age, after centuries of Western individualism. In other words, solitariness is not the whole truth about man: it must be completed by reference to our togetherness. It is not, therefore, beyond the bounds of our comprehension that there should exist in God something that corresponds to this togetherness. Sheer lone isolation cannot be the whole truth about him. But just as the paradox of our own solitary-communal nature defies logical expression, so we cannot arrive at a simple expression of this nature of God. The doctrine of the Trinity, though clearly not designed by theologians expressly for this purpose, does provide a window into this deeper truth.

The Christian approaches this question from the central affirmation of his faith—the divine love. The essence of love is self-giving. It is outgoing, the opposite of isolation. If, then, we say that God is love we suggest an activity directed towards someone. " God so loved the world that he gave . . ." Yes, but does that mean that the inhabited world must always have existed to be an object for God's love? To say so would contradict our belief in Creation and make the created as eternal as the Creator. The doctrine of the Trinity delivers us from this dilemma, and gives added richness and content to our thinking about God. " As the Father hath loved me," said Jesus, " so have I loved you." [1] The love of the Father for the Son is eternal in the being of God, and that love is the Holy Spirit. In other words, love can exist eternally in the one God because he is three Persons.

[1] St. John xv. 9.

Such thoughts are not easy to put into words. When we try to do so we sympathize with the prophet when he cried: "Verily thou art a God that hidest thyself, O God of Israel, the Saviour." Yet we can come to see why, just because of this "hiddenness" of God, the doctrine of the Trinity is a more satisfactory instrument for our minds than that of an undifferentiated unity. God is one; yes, but within that unity there lies also the origin of what we have glimpsed of the community of love.

Some Christians feel that any kind of speculation on the being of God is unprofitable, and that it is irrelevant, if not impious, to pursue the thought of Trinity into realms far beyond human experience. It is true that the doctrine comes to us, as we have seen, out of the Christian encounter with God. It is by his actions that we know him. Yet it is important to realize that when we say "Father, Son, and Holy Ghost" we are not just talking about different phases of God's activity. This way of thinking has led in the past to fantasies such as the theory that God acted as Father in Old Testament times, as Son in the New Testament, and as Holy Spirit today. And not a few modern Christians have a notion that God operates, as it were, in three disguises. We sometimes hear it suggested that the Holy Trinity is merely a way of using three names for the one God, according to the way we are thinking of him. But the New Testament dares to speak of the love of the Father for the Son "before the foundation of the world", and of our having "through him (Christ) access by one Spirit unto the Father"—suggesting throughout that the one God is eternal Trinity.

It is this truth that the Church has tried to preserve by the use of the words: three Persons, one

God. Unfortunately the word " person " can be most misleading. It suggests to most modern minds an " individual ", a separate personality, so that the Trinity is almost inevitably pictured as a kind of divine committee of three. It might almost have been better if the Church, for her formularies, had retained the Greek word " hypostasis ", which was specifically designed to express what is meant by the existence of the Father, the Son, and the Holy Spirit, within the unity of the Godhead. " Hypostasis " would have the advantage of being meaningless to all except those who troubled to study the doctrine, whereas " person " is deceptively familiar. Originally it was selected as the Latin word (*persona*) most adequate to translate " hypostasis ", and retained a technical theological meaning until it passed into common speech as a useful word to express an individual human being. In theological writings, as we can see from a glance at the Athanasian Creed, it retained the way of expressing the distinctness of being as contrasted with the unity of " substance ". However impatient we may become with theological definitions of this kind, and however theology may have to use in the future terms drawn from a different philosophical background, we have to accept the fact that there is, up to the present, no other way of saying what Christians feel must be said about their God—that he is three Persons in one Being.

Preachers on Trinity Sunday have combed creation to find helpful analogies for our thinking on this matter. Everything from the shamrock to depth psychology has been pressed into service. It is doubtful if any really illuminating analogy can be found to that which is, by definition, unique; yet there is point in showing that the Christian creeds are not asking assent to that which it is totally beyond our minds to conceive.

It is true here, as always in the Christian Faith, that the most helpful illustrations of the ways of God are to be found in the realm of human personality. This is not, as has been emphasized before, because we " create God in our own image ", but simply because we must speak of God in the highest terms that we know. By refusing to " make him seem human " we may make him seem sub-human. The blessed word " anthropomorphism " is often flung around in such discussions as if to detect a human analogy in our language about God were to make it nonsensical. But the alternative to using human analogies is to use sub-human analogies. Provided we remember that we are attempting to speak about GOD and not Superman, illustrations drawn from our experience in human life are likely to be the most useful and helpful we can find. Jesus himself consistently used human analogies in his teaching about God, and from him we also learn the saving phrase: " How much more . . ." (" If ye then, being evil, know how to give good gifts unto your children: *how much more* shall your heavenly Father give the Holy Spirit to them that ask him? " [1])

There is certainly an interesting analogy to the Trinity to be discovered in our own personalities. We can follow this up as a guide to our thinking without accepting it as an adequate " explanation " of the doctrine.

We start with the obvious fact of our oneness. No matter how disintegrated my personality might appear under psychiatric investigation, no matter

[1] St. Luke xi. 13.

how divided my mind and confused my emotions, I am conscious of the one continuous centre of my existence—in fact, what I mean by " I ". And this " I ", which we take for granted as the basis of our existence, is the greatest mystery confronting human thought. It can never be made the object of our study, for it is permanently the subject. The world, other people, our bodies, our minds, our psychological make-up—all can be the object of scientific investigation; but never the " I " while it is doing the investigating. Our capacity for reflecting on the " I "—what we call our self-consciousness— is the nearest we can come to this investigation, but there is always the " I " which is doing the reflecting. And self-consciousness is itself one of the deepest mysteries of life. We can thus begin to appreciate that a divine " I ", a divine self-consciousness, must be something beyond the reaches of our understanding. If the unity of the " I " is infinitely complicated with us, how much more in the divine Being?

Within this " I " it is not difficult to distinguish three modes of being which offer some analogy to the " Persons " of the Trinity.

(1) First, there is what we might call " I-in-myself ". There is an " I " whom no one else can fully know. Most of us as children were already conscious of this private self, this area where no other could penetrate. It is this inner citadel that really determines our being. When we find a person apparently without such an inner, uncommunicated self (of course, no one is without it) we are inclined to write them off as having " no personality ". " I-in-myself " means that area of my life for which I alone am responsible, in which my own decisions are taken. It is the element of solitariness which belongs

to all human personality. We discover this in our-selves as small children, and it is one of the dawning mysteries of life when we discover this in other people too. We find that our parents have a life of their own, which is not entirely concerned with ours; that friends have these hidden selves which makes them often strange and unpredictable.

There is a sense in which we can think of God the Father as God-in-himself. We are reminded that God also has this life of his own. This is why we are told that " no man hath seen God at any time ".[1] It is not given to man to see into the hidden life of God. Again we are told: " It is not for you to know the times or the seasons, which the Father hath put in his own power." [2] This life of God the Father is not something about which we can make statements—except that there is such a life. We are continually tempted to think of God as being wholly concerned with us, or with his universe—as if he were entirely contained therein. It is helpful to think of God the Father as God-in-himself, God in the inner mystery of his being. This will prevent us imagining that we can simply add up all that we know of God and say: This is the divine Being. We cannot do that with other people whom we know: how much more should we guard against such assumptions about God?

(2) Then there is the " I " that other people get to know. I do not remain " in-myself ". By words and actions I reveal myself, give myself away to others. This is what I am doing at the moment when I write this book. The printed words reveal something of what is in my mind, and incidentally reveal something of me. Every day of our lives we

[1] I John iv. 12.   [2] Acts i. 7.

communicate ourselves in one way or another. In deep friendship, and above all in marriage, this self-revelation reaches its profoundest levels. By unconscious acts we " give ourselves away ", as we say, but the greatest self-giving is our deliberate choice. We never ultimately confuse " I-in-myself " with " I-revealed ". The possibility of hypocrisy is a permanent reminder of how different they may be; yet the true person is one in whom there is an entire continuity between the inner self and that which is revealed. With such people we are sure, though we can never dare to claim a direct knowledge of their inner selves, that there is no inconsistency with what is revealed to us.

The Bible is, as we have already noted, a documentary record of men's meeting with God-revealed. Unless there was that in God which corresponded to this human self-communication we could have no knowledge of him at all. And as words are a symbol of our means of revealing ourselves it was natural for the prophets to describe God's revelation as " The Word of the Lord ". But the climax of the Biblical story of this revelation we know to be the " Word made flesh ". Jesus Christ is God's perfect communication of himself to men. " No man hath seen God at any time; *the only begotten Son, which is in the bosom of the Father, he hath declared him.*" [1] Again we can trace the distinction within the unity. God remains God. The Father is still unseen. Yet the Son reveals him. " He that hath seen me hath seen the Father." [2] And since we are now speaking of God, and not of men with all their fallibilities and hypocrisies, we can be sure that there is an entire consistency between what God is in himself and what

[1] St. John i. 18.   [2] St. John xiv. 9.

he has revealed. This has practical importance for the Christian life, since the misleading suggestion has sometimes been made that, although Christ is merciful, there may be lurking in the shadows a God of another aspect into whose clutches we may fall. God-revealed is not God-in-himself; yet they are one God, and utterly self-consistent.

(3) It is not fanciful to distinguish another way in which we exist in the mystery of our " I ". There is not simply " I-in-myself" plus " I-revealed ". There is the actual affecting of this communication. I may be revealing myself now in this printed page, but unless it is actually being communicated to you we are not in contact. The spark of communication must leap the barrier of two personalities whenever two of us meet, whether through books, letters, or conversation. This is just what we mean when we talk about someone's " spirit ". When we say " He's in the right spirit " we mean that we are in real communication. When we speak of the good " spirit " in a meeting we really mean that a living contact of person with person was taking place. By my spirit, then, I convey the " I-revealed " to another. And this spirit of mine is unconfined: it is remarkably independent of my bodily presence.

We have seen how the Holy Spirit is God in action in this way. " God-revealed ", God the Son, becomes real to us as his Spirit makes the contact. This is not another god, but the same God who exists in himself, and has revealed himself in Jesus Christ. By his Spirit he bridges time and space and is present to us as the living, sustaining, saving God. This is the point at which we actually meet with the one who has existed in himself from all eternity, and in Jesus Christ declared himself fully to all mankind.

E

God the Father; God the son; and God the Holy Spirit—one God. "I-in-myself"; "I-revealed"; my "spirit"—one "I". The analogy is suggestive, and helps us to see why the Christian Church has not been content with anything less than the doctrine of the Trinity to express the being of the God whom it worships.

Worship, however, is the important word. The Trinity is continually spoken of in churches, not to provide a stimulation for our minds, but as an invocation to worship. The Christian life can be described too exclusively in terms of its ethical fruits. The chief end of man, according to the Shorter Catechism, is " to glorify God and enjoy him for ever ". When people say, " What is the point in the doctrine of the Trinity? ", they probably mean, " What does it tell me to do? " But if our supreme task is to glorify God and enjoy him for ever a doctrine can be of fundamental importance without having any immediately obvious ethical content. In Biblical religion worship and life are never separated, and there is no trace of a purely æsthetic worship or sheer mysticism. Yet continually we find worship set in the forefront, as the chief activity of man from which all else must flow.

The vision of Isaiah in the Temple at Jerusalem is a notable example of this. The young prophet was drawn out in an ecstasy of worship as he realized the presence of God : " Holy, holy, holy, is the Lord of hosts : the whole earth is full of his glory." Then, after his experience of penitence and cleansing, comes the directly practical note : " Whom shall I send? " comes the voice of God. " Then said I, Here am I ; send me." [1] Before the kind of activity

[1] Isaiah vi. 8.

that we tend to think all-important is in view, the emphasis is simply and exclusively on the worship of God.

The kind of worship inspired by the Christian Faith is ultimately determined by belief in the Triune God. This conception is rich enough to satisfy the needs of the worshipping spirit. Nearly every sensitive man or woman who has experienced the worship of the Christian Church has known moments of awe and adoration called forth by the invocation of Father, Son, and Holy Spirit. These are of greater moment than any cold-blooded analysis of the doctrine in the study. The demand for a simple, readily understandable, doctrine of God may well come from our modern incapacity for worship, as well as from an inadequate thinking through of the meaning of " God ". It is not accidental that the Trinity has been the inspiration of major Christian art—in music, poetry, painting, and architecture. The artist instinctively recognizes the truth of that which lies beyond logical syllogisms. He finds in this Christian teaching a way of approach to God, a sense of God's approach to him, in which deep speaks unto deep.

The God whom we know as Father, Son, and Holy Spirit is a God in action. And the name of that action is love. Worship cannot be truly directed to some static ideal, or an empty unity. It is elicited by that which moves towards us, the dynamism of the God who is Father, Son, and Holy Spirit. The Christian believes that to respond in love to this God in adoration and praise is the basis of all true human action. To worship the Christian God is to be caught up into the life of the Trinity, to be drawn into the eternal love of the Father and the Son through the power of the Holy Spirit. This primary action of man is open to us wherever we are and at any time. But it is specifically provided for in the worship of the Church, where the family of God in their togetherness respond to the Trinity of love. And from that central point of worship the Church is summoned to move out into the world, to the total individual and social life of humanity, teaching and baptizing " in the name of the Father, and of the Son, and of the Holy Ghost ".

For further reading:

  " The Doctrine of the Trinity ": L. Hodgson.
  " The Mind of the Maker ": Dorothy Sayers.

CHAPTER VII

CHURCH AND SACRAMENTS

A<small>T</small> first sight there is something rather odd in the inclusion of " The Church " among the items of Christian belief. Yet it appears in the Apostles' Creed immediately after " I believe in the Holy Ghost ". It hardly seems to be the same *kind* of belief. We should rather expect the Church to be regarded as the body that does the believing than to be itself an object of faith. We can hardly imagine any other society including a belief in itself among the items of its creed. If, for instance, we were to found a Flat-Earth Society tomorrow with a creed to which all members would adhere it would certainly include the clause " I believe that the earth is flat ", but hardly one that read " I believe in the Flat-Earth Society ". Our difficulty with this point suggests that there is a very widespread misconception of what the Church really is. We tend to think of it as a group of people voluntarily associated for the furtherance of the Christian Faith.

That this is the usual way of thinking of the Church appears from one of the commonest questions that is asked today at Missions, question-panels, discussion groups, or wherever religious topics are ventilated : " Can I not be a Christian without joining the Church ? " On the analogy of other human societies and institutions the answer would appear to be : " Yes ". I can certainly believe that the earth is flat without attaching myself to any Flat-Earth Society. The Society would enable me to meet like-minded people and perhaps help to bolster up my waning faith from time to time, but I could ignore it completely and continue to believe in possibly a flatter earth than anyone else. Can I not, then, hold the major doctrines of the Christian Creed and practise the Christian life without having anything to do with the Christian Church?

It is not enough to answer this question with the peremptory claim that the Church is the sole custodian of Christianity, and therefore has the right to restrict the title " Christian " to those within its fold. This is bound to provoke the retort " Which Church? " and lead to endless discussion on ecclesiastical pedigree. It would be better to begin by admitting that the condition of the Church today has made such a question inevitable, and by a sympathetic understanding of the person who honestly desires to be a Christian but finds little that seems either helpful or useful in the activities of the local St. Vitus or Muggleton Memorial. We seem to have come to a stage in our spiritual history when thousands of disillusioned agnostics and humanists are finding themselves drawn to the Christian Faith with almost as much force as they are repelled by the Christian Church. If the answer to their question must be " No; you cannot be a Christian without being a member of the Church ", then a very careful explanation of what we mean by the Church is called for, which means in the end a justification of our including it among the other items of the Creed.

Before embarking on such an explanation there are, however, two preliminary points that ought to be raised in answer to this question.

(1) The man or woman who claims to be able to

believe and live as a Christian " outside the Church " is forgetting that none of us receives an individual private revelation of Christianity. We have all derived our knowledge of the Faith directly or indirectly from the Church. The Holy Spirit does indeed speak to the individual man or woman and bring faith to life, but our knowledge of God and of his Son is not imparted by any kind of private pipeline. We have received it from others, who received it from others, who received it from others . . . , which is another way of saying that our Christian knowledge is derived from the Church, the community which has existed from the beginning. Everyone who claims to be living a Christian life apart from the Church is actually living on capital that belongs to the Church. If there had been no continuing tradition of the Church we could know nothing of this Christianity, short of a miraculous intervention of God on our behalf. It is strange how often when someone says, " I don't need the Church: I have my own ideas on these matters ", these ideas turn out to be a pallid reflection of the teaching of the Church.

(2) It can be easily demonstrated from the New Testament that the possibility of being a lone Christian isolated from the fellowship was ruled out from the beginning. It might be truer to say that such an idea could never have entered the heads of the apostles. Religion everywhere was a social as well as a personal matter, and nowhere more than in the Jewish–Christian tradition. In the earliest days to be a Christian, to be baptized, to be a member of the Church were not successive steps but different ways of describing the same thing. The first converts on the day of Pentecost were " added to the

Church ", and it would have been inconceivable for anyone to have contracted out. This membership of the Church was part of what it meant to be a Christian. It was not an optional proceeding, depending on whether or not the new convert wanted to associate himself with the community. His re-birth, his baptism, was a birth into the Church. The communal aspect of Christianity was as essential a part of it as the individual. It has only been with the development of the idea of the separate, self-contained personality, now seen to be an aberration in human thought, that the notion of private Christianity could have arisen. Thus, while it is possible that one may say " I am a Christian, but I cannot feel at home in any modern denomination ", to say " I am a Christian, but have nothing to do with the Church " is a contradiction in terms.

For our understanding of the nature of the Church, then, we must begin by discarding the notion that it is a mere grouping of people who happen to hold similar religious convictions. It is integral to the Christian Faith. Everything written in these pages, however individual in its expression, arises out of the life of the Church. Theology is a function of the Church. Prayer, even when we enter into the private room and shut the door, is never a private activity. And the act of faith by which we are joined to the Spirit of life is not what the mystics have called " the flight of the alone to the alone ". " There is no other way of entering into life ", says Calvin, " unless she [the Church] conceive us in the womb, and give us birth."

For our understanding of this centrality of the Church in Christian faith we have to dig deeper than the surface truth that all religion has its social as well as individual aspect. We have to begin where the Bible begins—with the notion of " the people of God ". If the Bible can be simply described as the record of conversations between God and man it is clearly not simply a symposium of individual encounters. Our habit of reading little extracts from Scripture has encouraged us to think in terms of God's dealings with an Abraham, a Moses, an Isaiah, a Peter, or a Paul—and to forget that these individuals form part of a pattern in which God is forming a " people " for himself. The word " Israel " means " people of God ", and this is what the Old Testament is about. We miss the point, for instance, in the story of Abraham, if we see in it simply an example of one man's adventures with God —and even more, if we treat it as a segment of the Semitic folklore of a nomadic age. It is recorded as the founding of the nation that was to be God's chosen people—not God's " favourites ". They were to be the family of God, living in obedience to his law, and shedding his light to the world around. " In thee shall all the families of the earth be blessed."

The rest of the Old Testament is the story of this people and their destiny. Under Moses and his successors they are hammered into a self-conscious nation with the law of God as their guiding-star. The rites and ceremonies of their cultus, the psalms they sang, the turbulent history under successive kings, the thunderings of the prophets are all recorded for us as phases in the story of a people who have a special covenant with God. On the whole it is a tragic story. Israel, as a whole, is seen to have failed in its mission. Yet the idea is indestructible. Even at the worst time of national declension the prophets spoke of a " remnant " who were still the true Israel, the real people of God. And in the bitter experience of exile there dawned the conviction that perhaps God's people were to prevail in the world not by material success or force of arms, but through suffering and humble service. The Old Testament ends on a note of bewilderment trembling with expectancy. The covenant stands; the promise of God is sure. But how is his purpose to be fulfilled in this battered wreckage of the people of God? What is the Hope of Israel?

In such a gallop through the Old Testament we must by-pass much that is relevant to our understanding of the Church. But it may be enough to indicate how fundamental is the idea of the divine community. Thus when Jesus was born he was cradled in this " people of God ". This is the significance of the Hebrew songs which St. Luke's Gospel offers as the setting of his birth.[1] " He hath holpen his servant Israel, in remembrance of his mercy; as he spake to our fathers, to Abraham, and to his seed for ever." " Blessed be the Lord God of Israel; for he hath visited and redeemed his people." We sometimes forget that Jesus had this background and that his entire ministry was within the framework of Israel.

When he set out on his short and decisive mission his first step was to constitute a community around him, an inner circle of " disciples ". It is not accidental that twelve was also the number of the tribes of Israel. If we read the Gospels with this understanding of the Old Testament it becomes more and more apparent that Jesus was deliberately fulfilling the destiny of Israel—and meant men to

[1] St. Luke i.

see it. This may well be one of the reasons why he so often referred to himself as " the Son of Man ", for this term had already been used to describe Israel—the people of God. If the purpose of God in choosing Israel was to have an instrument for the fulfilment of his will on earth, then we see this purpose concentrated and effected in Christ. " Then said I, Lo, I come (in the volume of the book it is written of me,) to do thy will, O God." [1] That, at any rate, was how the author of the Epistle to the Hebrews interpreted the story.

There is a curious sense of a narrowing-down of the people of God in these Scripture records. Israel, itself a small and insignificant fraction of the world's population, was chosen to reveal the way and obey the will of God among men. When Israel fails a Remnant is left, and it is to the remnant of this Remnant that Jesus comes at the beginning of our era. He draws around him the little band of twelve men, saying: " Fear not, little flock; for it is your Father's good pleasure to give you the Kingdom." [2] But even the " little flock " are scattered, and in the end Jesus is left alone. At Calvary the disciples have forsaken him and have fled. The people of God has narrowed down to this One. And on the Cross he represents, not a lone martyr, victim of a judicial murder, but quite clearly the people of God, the Servant of God upon whom is laid " the iniquity of us all ".[3]

That this is not a fanciful reading of the events is clear from the continued emphasis in the New Testament on the representative nature of Christ's life, action, and passion. The " for us " which we have already noted carried with it the thought of a Christ

[1] Hebrews x. 7.   [2] St. Luke xii. 32.   [3] Isaiah liii. 6.

who incorporates in himself a whole people. And, exactly as the love of God seemed to have been defeated when Jesus died, so the plan for a " people of God " seemed finally frustrated when this Son of Man perished. Yet again the answer is to be found in the Resurrection and the subsequent events.

The narrowing-down of the people of God gives place to an opening-out. Christ rises from the dead, and his followers are immediately drawn to him. He appears to them not only singly but as a group. This group is seen clinging timidly together until the day of Pentecost. Then with a swift and decisive movement, reflected in the burning words of the report, the disciples knew themselves to be united with their Lord—and re-constituted as the people of God. This was precisely the phrase they came to use. They were the " new Israel ".

The origins of the word " Church " are much disputed, but it seems certain that the first Christians used the word " ecclesia " in the Old Testament sense of the " people of God ". (It was the word used for this purpose in the Greek translation of the Old Testament.) It is important to note that they did not use it primarily in the sense of a local community, like a synagogue. From the beginning they knew themselves to be called into a new community. There is no trace of a decision to *found* such a community. The people of God had always existed. They had, as it were, died into Jesus Christ—and now all who were united with him were the new, the risen, the empowered Israel. As this people of God went into action they found it hard to distinguish Christ and his Church. Converts were not won to an isolated " decision for Christ ". They preferred to say: " The Lord added to the Church daily such as should be saved." [1] And the Book of the Acts recounts the still unfinished story of how this people of God expands into all the world.

We can better understand how the Church comes to be an article of faith rather than a mere description of a Christian organization when we realize the meaning of this conception of a people of God and how closely Christ is identified with it. The Church is not an after-thought: it is the family of God that he planned from the beginning, and into which he seeks to draw all mankind. This is why it is described in the Creed as " holy ": its founder is God not man. And the Christian Church, unlike the former " people of God ", is not a national community, but a supra-national one. In the New Testament we see the preparatory stage of a " national covenant " transcended, and the new Israel proclaimed as the world-wide family of God in which " there is neither Jew nor Greek, there is neither bond nor free, there is neither male nor female: for ye are all one in Christ Jesus ".[2] This is why it is described in the Creed as " Catholic " (although the word came to have later associations with the idea of traditional doctrines maintained against the emerging heresies). When the Church is also described as "Apostolic" we are reminded that those who laid the earthly foundations and established " churches " at Jerusalem, Antioch, Athens, Ephesus, and throughout the Roman Empire were the apostles—the eye-witnesses of Christ's Resurrection.

It is clear that the first Christians believed in *one* Church. This one Church had local existence in the form of churches at Corinth, Ephesus, Philippi,

[1] Acts ii. 47.   [2] Galatians iii. 28.

and elsewhere, but there is nothing in the New Testament to correspond to our modern denominations. This one Church was not just an idea—in the sense in which a modern cynic has said, " I believe in One Holy Catholic Church—and regret that it doesn't exist." Christians sometimes take refuge in the idea of the " Church invisible " to explain the essential unity that underlies our outward divisions, but the one Church of the New Testament was perfectly visible. Men could see its congregations in action, its leaders moving from church to church, its councils taking concrete decisions, its tremendous tensions being held in the unity of the Spirit. Paul's answer to the splintering tendency which soon shows itself in any movement was short and incisive: " Is Christ divided? " [1] The Church has its unity in Christ, and as Christ became flesh so the one Church must be clothed in the flesh and blood of common life.

The organic relationship of Christ to his Church appears in the New Testament metaphors used to describe it. The Church is a building of which Christ is the foundation. The Church is a bride of whom Christ is the bridegroom. The Church is a body whose head is Christ. There is nothing to parallel this kind of relationship between a founder of a religion and the religious community. A Jew would never speak like this about Moses and the Israelites; nor a Muslim of Mohammed and Islam. The metaphor of the body is in many ways the most revealing. A body exists to be the means of expression for the spirit. We can talk this way without being committed to any dualism about man being body plus spirit: rather he is body/spirit. Jesus

[1] I Corinthians i. 13.

had a real human body as the instrument for his Spirit, the Holy Spirit. Through this body, by this body, he moved, talked, suffered, healed, carried on his mission. When his body was no longer seen, not even in its resurrection appearance, the disciples were at a loss. But, as we have seen, the day of Pentecost brought them the burning conviction that he was still alive among them. His Spirit possessed them. What about the body? That, too, was given back to men on that same day. For the Church, the group of men and women who were united to Christ in his Spirit, was the new body to be the instrument of Christ's work on earth. This is the only way in which we can understand that strange word when Jesus said to his disciples: "He that believeth on me, the works that I do shall he do also; and greater works than these shall he do; because I go unto my Father." [1] The disciples were to do even greater works—in the sense that now the Spirit of Christ was liberated from the geographical limitation of his earthly body and free to work through this new body throughout the entire world and all time to come.

The Church, then, has on it the marks of its Lord— the divine become human, the Word made flesh. On the one hand, the Church is a divine society, owing its origin to God, and ruled by Christ the only Head. On the other hand, it is thoroughly human, incarnated in a thousand congregations, committees, missions, financial statements, cathedrals, mothers' meetings, hymn-books, mission-hospitals— all the necessary machinery of human activity. This dual nature has belonged to the Church from the beginning. As we have already noted, the first

[1] St. John xiv. 12.

chapter in the Church's history—the Book of the Acts, Chapter Three—begins with the " sound from heaven " and ends with the selling and sharing of this world's goods.

It is in this context that we can understand the significance of the sacraments. The idea of a sacrament is generally and easily understood. Every community has been accustomed to use material symbols to convey a spiritual truth. A national flag or an engagement-ring are obvious examples. Religions of all kinds have made special use of this " sacramental " approach. Altars, idols, incense, charms, vestments have all been used to convey in varying degrees spiritual truths or benefits through material objects. Yet the Christian use of the word " sacrament " conveys a more precise and powerful meaning. In a general sense the entire Christian outlook can be said to be " sacramental " in that it rests upon the conviction that God himself entered the material world in Christ—that the Word was made flesh. And the Church has for this reason its " sacramental " nature as a human organization of flesh and blood through which we are summoned to partake in the divine community. But the Church has always attached supreme significance to two sacramental rites in which this truth becomes luminous and efficacious for the believer—Baptism and the Lord's Supper.

These two sacraments are marked off from all other sacramental ceremonies in that, not only were they founded by Christ himself, but they are the means of our union with him in the Church. Baptism is the sacrament of entrance; the Lord's Supper the sacrament of continual communion. They are thus integral to the life of the Church, expressing and conveying the benefits of Christ to his people.   In spite of the great divergences of belief that have arisen within the Church as to the exact meaning of these sacraments, all who use them would agree that they are the expression of our union with Christ in his Church.   Throughout the Christian centuries the water, the bread, and the wine have been the means whereby men, women, and children have been united in faith with their Lord within the fellowship of the Church.   When the first Christian sermon was ended and the people asked, " What shall we do? " Peter's answer was quite specific: " Repent, and be baptized every one of you in the name of Jesus Christ." [1] And when the first Christians came together they heard the Lord's words, " Take, eat: this is my body, which is broken for you ",[2] and so entered into communion with him—and with one another.   It is at this point—where water is poured, bread eaten, wine drunk—that the material life of the Church is seen to be the flash-point of the divine.

This, then, is the Church in which Christians believe.   It is a society of which Christ is Head, existing in every corner of the world to worship, to work, and to witness by his Spirit.   It is thoroughly divine in origin and destiny; thoroughly human in its living expression.   Its purpose is Christ's purpose—to draw mankind into the family of God.   Its methods must be his methods—not force, but the love of God expressed in preaching, teaching, worship, healing, service.   As a divine society its boundaries are known only to God. Jesus warned more than once that some who think they are within it are really outside; while others

---

[1] Acts ii. 38.   [2] 1 Corinthians xi. 24.

F

regarded as outside are really within it. For the true Church can be nothing other than the Kingdom of God. Yet as a visible society of men and women its boundaries are more clearly drawn, and from the beginning the Church has exercised a discipline of inclusion and exclusion. The way to Church membership is through the acceptance of this discipline. There is no short-cut to a purely " spiritual " Church, any more than there was a way for the disciples to be secret followers of a " spiritual " Jesus when he stood before them in flesh and blood and made his claim upon them. Anyone today who wants to be united with Christ in the fellowship of his people must find his way to the local visible embodiment of his Church. The alternative to being a member of a modern denomination is to excommunicate oneself; for the Church as a concrete institution exists and cannot be ignored.

The multiplicity of denominations is undoubtedly a cause of confusion to the modern enquirer. Yet it is possible to exaggerate the points of difference and forget the beliefs on which they are united over against the unbelieving world. There has seldom been a time when Christians of all traditions have been more ardently seeking to realize their true unity in Christ. This modern movement—known as " ecumenical " from the Greek word signifying the inhabited earth—is not simply a shrewd attempt to combine forces in an emergency, but a steady seeking to find that visible unity which is Christ's clear will for his Church. No section of the Church is guiltless in this matter of division, and through penitence and prayer a unity is being sought which will be other than the " spiritual union " which many unthinkingly accept as a sufficient substitute, and yet not the unity of a " power-Church " imposing uniformity by means of a centralized ecclesiastical bureaucracy.

It is easy to see how divisions in the Church have come about. Already in the infant Corinthian Church St. Paul noted the tendency for groups to form: " I am of Paul; and I of Apollos; and I of Cephas; and I of Christ." [1] Strong personalities can cause disruption, and the party-spirit is seldom absent from any community. Differences of understanding in doctrine can lead Christians to divide for conscience' sake. Nor need it be assumed that divisions are always caused by those who make their protest against the doctrine or practice of the contemporary Church. The tendency to corruption and petrification which is always latent in any Church is itself a major cause of schism. Then there are the inevitable temperamental differences among Christians which lead some to seek ceremony, liturgical worship, rules of life; while others seek plain forms and the maximum of individual freedom. Many of the historic divisions in the Church stem from disagreement on the method of Church government. In the New Testament there is no clear instruction on this point, and the rival systems, for instance, of Episcopacy, Presbyterianism, and Independency, have all claimed Scriptural warrant. One of the signs of hope in the present situation is the growing willingness of all parts of Christendom to recognize that Christ is active in his Church in more ways than each section used to consider possible.

There are two pairs of complementary truths about the Church which help us to sort out these

[1] I Corinthians i. 12.

divergences and point towards a fuller understanding of its nature.

The first is that the Church possesses both *continuity* and *vitality*.

When we were considering how the Holy Spirit makes the work of Christ contemporary for us, we saw that another way in which we are linked to these decisive acts of two thousand years ago is through the continuity of the Church. The apostles were the eye-witnesses, and they committed their knowledge to others, who in their turn passed it on. This process is described in the apostolic word to the younger Timothy: " And the things that thou hast heard of me among many witnesses, the same commit thou to faithful men, who shall be able to teach others also." [1]   The knowledge of Christ and his saving work was passed on in the fellowship of the Church. Through the ages the Church has maintained the continuity of this message in its theology, and in its worship, by word and sacrament. One of the instruments for this continuity has been the ministry. In every age men have been set aside for the conduct of worship, the study of Scripture, pastoral care of a congregation, and the administration of the sacraments. When we think of this continuity our picture of the Church is rather like that of a river of divine grace flowing through history into which we can be launched, knowing that the waters beneath us have flowed unbroken from the Christian source.

Those who stress this element of continuity in their thinking of the Church will tend to be traditionalists. They will want to emphasize everything that guarantees a pure succession, and will be suspicious

[1] II Timothy ii. 2.

of innovation. Ecclesiastical pedigree will be all-important, and creeds and constitutions sacrosanct. Ministerial orders and the maintenance of ancient liturgy will be of supreme importance.

There is, however, the other element in the Church's life, which may be called its vitality. By this term is meant the life-giving link of the Church in every age with its Lord through the Spirit. To use the fashionable geometrical terminology, while continuity represents the horizontal life of the Church, vitality represents the vertical. Or, we may say that while some think of the life of the Church as a " river of grace ", others tend more naturally to think of a fountain springing up new in every age. There is a sense in which the Church comes to life moment by moment in the power of the Spirit and is thus guided into new truth and action. When we think in this way we realize that to " hold fast the form of sound words, which thou hast heard of me " [1] may not be so essential as being " in the Spirit on the Lord's day ".[2]

Those who stress this element of vitality are less concerned with the questions of succession and doctrinal tradition. They believe in the prophetic word rather than in sacramental continuity. The present contact of the Church with its Lord seems to them more important than its lineage. In the ministry they will seek inspiration rather than valid succession.

It will be easily seen how this tendency to stress either continuity or vitality must lead to divisions, based partly on temperament and partly on genuine understandings or misunderstandings of the Gospel. The most hopeful sign in the current discussions that

[1] II Timothy i. 13. [2] Revelation i. 10.

are taking place between sundered parts of the Church is a recognition growing on all sides that both elements are essential to the life of the Church. Without continuity there is no guarantee of an apostolic succession in the sense that every Christian must value, no protection against fanatical deviation, and an impoverishment of worship consequent on the loss of the " communion of saints ".   Without vitality the Church must lapse into a cold traditional formalism, and is cut off from the renewing and reforming power of the Spirit.   To believe in one holy, catholic, and apostolic Church is to be committed to the family of God which is united with its Lord both in the continuity of its life from the beginning and in the vitality of its contact with his Spirit now.

The second pair of complementary truths about the Church deals with the relation of the Church to the world.

Every Christian experiences at some point the tensions involved in being at the same time a member of the Church and a member of a more or less secular state.   He is a citizen of the Kingdom of God and also a citizen of a kingdom whose laws are different.   He knows himself called to live in the environment of eternity, but is aware that he is deeply involved in temporal affairs.   He has duties as a Church member, but he has also duties as a citizen.   The classic example of this dilemma is set by the Gospel incident when Jesus was asked if it were lawful to pay tribute to Cæsar or not.   His answer, " Render therefore unto Cæsar the things which are Cæsar's ; and unto God the things that are God's ",[1] makes it quite clear that the Christian cannot con-

[1] St. Matthew xxii. 21.

tract out of this world and its responsibilities, but leaves the question open as to where the line is to be drawn between the two spheres. This is, of course, entirely consistent with his refusal to be a legislator and the nature of the Christian life. No code of conduct can be elaborated which will infallibly distinguish between the rights of Cæsar and of the Church.

The Biblical way of stating this problem is to say that the Christian is *in* the world but not *of* it. The Church shares to the full in the life of this world, but its roots and destiny are beyond it. To say exactly on each occasion which of these two truths should be stressed by the Church or the Christian is as difficult as finding a formula to express the divine-human nature of Christ. For the former problem springs from the latter.

One strong trend in the Church's history derives its power from the knowledge that it is not *of* this world. "We ought to obey God rather than men"[1] was the way they put it in the earliest days. The early Church—a tiny minority in a thoroughly pagan environment—was naturally conscious of the other-worldly basis of its life. Relations with the state were tense and often tragic. Echoes of this period of strain are to be found in some of the Epistles and in the Book of Revelation, and the writings of the Fathers show how the Church was continually struggling to maintain its life in face of hostile powers. The situation changed almost overnight with the settlement under Constantine, when Christianity suddenly became the recognized official religion of the Roman world. Yet even through and beyond that time there were those who continually sought to

[1] Acts v. 29.

draw a sharp line between the Church and the world. The Roman Catholic Church provided for this kind of witness in the institution of the monastic orders who sought to be radically sundered from the world. Protestantism gave birth to many groups whose continual protest was against the absorption of the Church in the world, and this trend is today represented by all Churches who are acutely conscious of being a minority in a pagan environment. This emphasis is seen in strict rules of membership ("only the clearly converted"); a puritanical attitude to the pleasures of the world; a disavowal of any state connection; and sometimes even in a refusal of some of the duties of citizenship.

The other strong trend in the Church's life springs from the truth that it is *in* the world. Starting from the apostolic teaching that "the powers that be are ordained of God",[1] this conception of the Church naturally welcomed the "conversion" of the Roman Empire and gave birth to the idea of "Christendom" —a Church co-terminous with the state. The medieval period saw the triumph of this view, when to be a European was *ipso facto* to be a Christian—at least in theory. With the break-up of this pattern at the Renascence and Reformation the emergent nation-states each evolved its national Church, and so the idea was preserved to a greater or less degree. Today most of the major Churches in the Western world cling to some remnant of the Christendom-idea, and refuse to give up the notion of a "Christian state". They take seriously the Church's responsibility in the world, and claim the whole of national and international life as the sphere of the Church's concern.

---

[1] Romans xiii. 1.

This rough outline of two divergent streams of Christian thinking about the Church and its relation to the world will serve to show how the paradox of being " in the world but not of the world " [1] is responsible for conflicting views on many current questions. National establishment, pacifism, infant baptism, Sunday observance, resistance to the totalitarian state, Church discipline, education, and a host of other thorny problems are connected with this fundamental tension in the Church's life. Again, it looks as if the pressure of contemporary events in Church and state is enabling Christians to examine many of these questions in a new light. The stark divisions show signs of breaking down. Yet in the end it must be accepted that there is no possible blue-print for this world/Church relationship, no perfect adjustment for the life of the people of God in this world. To believe in the Church means, among other things, accepting the strains and stresses of life in the Christian community in an alien world. St. Paul's greeting to the Roman Christians " To all that be in Rome, beloved of God, called to be saints " still holds good for the Church today. " *In Rome . . . called to be saints.*" [2]

The Christian Faith includes the Church. The Christ who reveals the Father, who delivers man, who is alive by his Spirit today, meets us in the community of his people. That community is, looked at from one angle, a struggling, sinning, divided, ineffective institution—not sure how far it is at home in this world. From the other angle it is the divine community, nurse of saints and martyrs, fount of a vast power of healing and teaching and reconciling ministry, a fellowship of the Spirit, whose head is

[1] St. John xvii. 15.　　[2] Romans i. 7.

Christ himself, in whom and to whom a continuous worship ascends from earth to heaven. It is man on the march to God.

For further reading:

" The Evangelical Church Catholic ": Carnegie Simpson.

" The Reunion of the Church ": Lesslie Newbigin.

CHAPTER VIII

THE DESTINY OF MAN

In a college at Brisbane I was once confronted by a group of about a hundred students who had been invited to ask me questions about anything at all. The first question was " What do the students in Edinburgh do during Charities Week? " The last question—three hours later—was " What is the purpose of life? "

Sooner or later serious discussion on any subject will arrive at this ultimate question. Politics leads to it: so does art, ethics, sociology, sex—any region of human thought or activity will lead us in the end to ask what human life is all about, whether there is any goal to which we can move, or be moved, any meaning in the drama of history. Philosophy has been concerned with this question since the dawn of human thought, and the greatest literature of all languages has portrayed man grappling with his destiny. Yet there is a deep scepticism in many minds today as to whether any answer can be given— and, we may add, a shallow scepticism in many more. That is why the description of a philosopher as a man in a dark cellar looking for a black cat that isn't there is greeted with popular applause, re-doubled when it is added that a theologian is a man who claims to have found it.

The serious sceptic is one who has heard the philosophical debate, pondered the thought of dramatist, poet, and novelist, and given heed to the claims of religion—and yet is still groping. The shallow sceptic is one who rationalizes his desire to drift by the glib assertion that ultimate purpose is a " meaningless conception ", thus writing off the greatest productions of the spirit of man as much ado about nothing. Anyone who has reached this point in reading this book is clearly one who is prepared to take such questions seriously. There is every justification for a renewed quest after the *ends* of life at this period when scientific progress has placed *means* at our disposal beyond the dreams of our ancestors. A civilization equipped with the glittering machinery of technology without any clue as to what man is meant to be and to do is a gigantic shaggy-dog story, a kind of cosmic joke. In such an atmosphere it is vital that the Christian claims be heard and re-examined.

The preceding chapters have implied that human life is not accidental, or determined by mechanistic law, but that it is subject to a divine purpose. Man is free to co-operate with this purpose—or not. Christians believe that life receives its meaning from this God-given purpose. The answer to the first question of the Shorter Catechism puts it with superb precision: " Man's chief end is to glorify God, and to enjoy him for ever." When we can give content to these words we are in possession of a key to existence which, although it cannot open the doors to a final answer to theoretical conundrums, provides a motive for living and an entrance into a world of infinite variety and meaning.

Briefly, we may say that to glorify God is to respond to him as a son. In terms of the Gospel that means that our purpose in life is to become like *the* Son of God. And this process takes place within the family of God, which is his Church. The difficulty with such statements is that our human experience inclines us to limit the scope of this process, so that it almost sounds like saying that the mountains of history have laboured to produce the miserable mouse of a modern Christian. To understand the claim we have to expand our conception of the Christian life and the Christian Church to truly Biblical dimensions. We are not talking about conventional piety as the chief end of man, or of the withering of the fulness of life into the confines of the organized churches. We are referring to the " salvation " of which Scripture speaks, which is nothing less than the re-creation of mankind, in which a transformed humanity as the Body of Christ comes " in the unity of faith, and of the knowledge of the Son of God, unto a perfect man, unto the measure of the stature of the fulness of Christ ".[1] Such a goal includes the fruition of every human value, individual and social, so that every impulse of the human spirit towards the good, the true, and the beautiful is finally crowned with meaning.

The Christian idea of man's destiny is thus frankly supernatural. That is to say it does not find meaning and purpose simply within the process of nature or human nature. This world is part of another infinitely richer, fuller world which in the Christian tradition goes under the names of eternity, heaven, the Kingdom of God. This invisible world is part of the experience of the believer here and now. For God has revealed himself, the powers of heaven have broken through, and from the central act of Christ's incarnation the eternal light shines backward and forward through history so that men within the frontiers of time and space may still be citizens of

[1] Ephesians iv. 13.

that richer world. (The impinging of the eternal world on this one is the real meaning of miracle in the Christian vocabulary. About every recorded miraculous event there are, of course, questions to be asked. How strong is the evidence? May this not have been a natural occurrence which has been given miraculous form? Is there any conceivable point in this story? But when all such legitimate questions have been asked about the miracles in the Christian story we are left with the clear impression that from the beginning there have been associated with the Church's life events which are unexplainable by natural causes. These are the " signs " of the eternal world within the present order. And since the entire Christian Faith depends on the supreme miracle of the Incarnation it is futile to cavil at the possibility of events which are beyond the normal experience of mankind.) It is by living within this extra dimension that we find the ultimate meaning and purpose of our life. The light by which we live " beacons from the abode where the eternals are "—or, to use more Biblical language, we exist on earth in order to do the will of our " Father in heaven ". We perhaps do not always realize that every time we pray " Thy will be done in earth, as it is in heaven " we are confessing that our lives here and now can and should be regulated by that eternal sphere in which God's will is perfectly accomplished.

Christianity is, of course, not the only faith that looks on our present life as conditioned by an invisible world. Long before the birth of Christ a picture of this kind had been beautifully drawn by Plato, and it has never ceased to captivate the philosophic mind, and inspire the poet and the painter. And the great religions of the East have implanted so deep a belief in the "world beyond" that to their millions of adherents our Western civilization, for all its Christian basis, looks crassly worldly and materialistic. We must now ask what it is that gives to the Christian Faith its unique insight and specific attitude to the problem of human destiny.

The religions of the world have sometimes been classed into those which are world-affirming and those which are world-denying. That is to say that some religions lay emphasis on the value of human life and the possibility of an almost unlimited improvement in the conditions under which man has to live, while other religions look on this life as a mere lethal chamber whose temporary attractions are utterly illusory and in which our only duty is to prepare ourselves for the life to come. The question is then asked: into which category can we put the Christian Faith? On the one hand, we can point to the story of Christian optimism and activism: the vast programme of social amelioration and scientific advancement prompted by the Christian instinct to accept and affirm the values of this world. On the other hand, we can adduce the evidence of Christian renunciation—the ascetic element in Catholicism and Protestantism which has constantly sought to renounce the values of this world in favour of the benefits of a world to come. Historically, we can see this dichotomy in terms of the contrast between Catholic monasticism and Protestant Puritanism on the one side, and the rollicking *bon-viveur* Chestertonian Catholicism and the activist Y.M.C.A. Protestantism on the other. In terms of the present day, we can take note of the contrast between

Christians who find their only hope in the return of Christ to bring history to an end, and those who see in the application of Christian principles a way of advancement towards the Kingdom of God on earth.

This contrast within the Christian Church indicates that in essence the Faith is neither world-affirming nor world-denying. It is *world-transforming*. As we have seen at every point in our discussion of Christian doctrine, we are not dealing with a system of ideas, but with an action of God upon our world—a saving, redeeming action. Therefore, although the Christian can by temperament be either optimistic or pessimistic, he is committed to a dynamic view of history, a belief that men and women can be transformed by God's Spirit and that mankind is " going somewhere ". There is an inescapable note of urgency in all authentic Christianity. " At my back I always hear, Time's wingèd chariot hurrying near." In other words, time is taken seriously: it is not regarded as a mere illusion from which we can escape into an eternal world.

In this Christianity is sharply divided off from all Eastern religion and classical philosophy. At a time when many are despairing of man's future it is natural that many of these religions and philosophies should make a renewed appeal to the human heart. For they virtually abandon the attempt to make sense of the human story in terms of a goal to be reached. For them history is either illusory or else it is a meaningless circular process. In either case salvation means an escape from the temporal world. For Buddhism and Hinduism there can be no Saviour who effects a once-for-all deliverance for mankind and to whom all history moves. There are many important parallels between these religions and Christianity, and the common terminology of sin and salvation may often suggest that they mean the same thing. But this difference is fundamental. The Christian believes that salvation is not to be found by turning away from this life in time, but by accepting it as the sphere of God's saving action in Jesus Christ and therefore the unique opportunity to seek his Kingdom and righteousness.[1] With this conviction goes the assurance of a decisive victory of good over evil, already effected in the Cross and Resurrection, and awaiting consummation at the end of time.

Christianity, then, has a doctrine of the End— and in both senses of the word. It is an end in the sense of a goal to be reached, a conviction which imparts the dynamic to the Church. It is also the end in the sense of a winding-up of the historical process, a conviction which imparts urgency and seriousness. It is this aspect of the Christian Faith that has been the mainspring of the civilization in which we live. The entire range of human progress in the Western world during the last two thousand years—in the fields of education, sociology, medicine, politics, and technology as well as in ethical behaviour—has been made possible by the power of this belief in the end. It has had its tragic repercussions as well as its spectacular triumphs. For wherever men take seriously their beliefs in a divine end to be pursued and the consequent necessity of action, divergence of view ceases to be an academic matter for interesting argument and becomes a life-or-death question which human perversity has often tried to settle by violence. It is not therefore

[1] St. Matthew vi. 33.

possible to speak unambiguously of the triumph of Christian principles in the story of our civilization. Yet everything that the spirit of man has wrought within that era—the astounding progress for which, in spite of its set-backs, we remain profoundly thankful—has been a direct consequence of Christian belief in an end to be pursued. Even the bitterest opponents of the Christian Faith have drawn the weapons of their attack from the armoury of Christian tradition, for they, too, have possessed the dynamic view of history and have held some conception of a Kingdom to be sought. Marxism, for instance, could scarcely have arisen in any other context than one dominated by the Biblical view of history.

The Christian doctrine of the End is technically known as " Eschatology ". Under that heading theologians have usually treated such subjects as heaven and hell, judgment, the Return of Christ, and the end of the world. This is an integral part of the Christian Faith, and not something to be dealt with in a postscript. As it is, however, one of the most controversial and bewildering subjects there is a constant temptation to by-pass it in popular expositions of the creeds. It is the more tempting to do so when we consider that the field of eschatology has been the happy hunting-ground of all manner of fanatical sects. A powerful fascination is exercised on certain minds by such topics as the future destiny of mankind, especially when they are served up with all the paraphernalia of mystic prophecy and quotations from the books of Daniel and Revelation. So many dogmatic statements have been made in this context about the future of this world and the life of the world to come that it is not surprising that a reverent agnosticism on the whole matter should have settled on a large section of the Church. It is, however, necessary to note what are the essential Christian truths which lie behind such creedal statements as " from whence he shall come to judge both the quick and the dead " and " the resurrection of the body and the life everlasting ".

First, it should hardly be necessary to say that the Christian Faith implies that there is a real life for mankind beyond the grave. The invisible world by which this world is conditioned is a world in which death has been vanquished. The victory wrought by Christ is no real victory for the believer unless he can share in the immortality which Christ has won, in the resurrection from the dead. We cannot miss the confidence of the apostles as recorded in the New Testament that death had been conquered. Resurrection from the dead was part of the meaning of union with Christ. As St. Paul put it, when faced with imminent death: " To me to live is Christ, and to die is gain." [1] Even more explicitly he wrote to the Corinthians that " if the dead rise not, then is not Christ raised ".[2] Union with Christ means that what happened to him will happen to us, for we share his life.

The Christian Faith bases its hope of life beyond the grave on this resurrection-faith. Many general arguments can be offered for a doctrine of immortality, but the Christian is concerned with the quality of such life, and that quality is described in terms of growth into Christ, an ever-fuller apprehension of the glory of God. There is no simple doctrine of the immortality of the soul to be found in the Bible. The word is Resurrection. The Old Testament contains only the vaguest references to a

[1] Philippians i. 21.   [2] I Corinthians xv. 16.

future life. By the time of the Incarnation there was a doctrine of Resurrection, but it was regarded by traditionalists, like the Sadducees, as an innovation. Jesus himself dealt with their objections with the word: " He is not the God of the dead, but of the living: for all live unto him." [1] We take this to mean that when a man or woman is laid hold of by God in this life he is not dropped into non-existence when physical death intervenes. He is raised to a new life, and thus remains for ever with God. When Jesus himself had died and risen again there was no doubt whatever in the minds of his disciples that because of their union with him they would be raised up again to share in the life of the world to come.

This, of course, leaves many questions unanswered. Before looking at some of these, it is right to stress again that the Christian hope includes without question or cavil a full personal renewal of life after death in that world beyond where God's will is done. Yet we must also note that there is the utmost reticence in the Scriptures about the nature of such a life. When Jesus answered the question of the Sadducees on this point he made it plain that it is totally impossible for us within the limitations of time and space to understand the nature of the life beyond. Books that speak of such conditions, like the Book of Revelation, are forced to speak in terms of imagery and myth. Nothing could be more misleading than to make Oriental symbolism the basis for exact material calculations as to the details of a future life. Therefore most churches today show a proper reticence in all questions of this kind. Conditions in this deeper dimension of living could no

[1] St. Luke xx. 38.

more be understandable by us now than would our three-dimensional lives be to a creature that was confined to a life of two dimensions. To convey to us the meaning of life free from the limitations of time and space would be more difficult than explaining the meaning of colour to one who was colour-blind.

The most that we have a right to believe in the light of the Gospel is that life beyond the grave is richer and fuller than this one, and that it consists in a continued growth into the image of Christ—together. We have no warrant for believing that it will consist in the kind of dreary uniformity suggested by some popular hymns. "In my Father's house are many mansions." [1] I cannot interpret these words in the sense of these grim rows of identical houses that modern Britain has spread around its suburbs. They suggest rather an infinite variety of spheres where the unique lives of each of God's children find mutual enrichment and fulfilment. Eternal life, according to the Bible, is knowledge of God—not endless time. It is a quality of life into which we enter now, and which finds its true flowering in a totally different environment. Anyone who is conscious of the small progress they have made in the years granted them in this world will gladly understand the need for another sphere in which they can continue to become the sons and daughters of God.

But what of those who have no knowledge of Christ, or have rejected his approach in this life? Is there, as the churches have taught, a place of punishment, a hell which is as eternal as heaven?

In the first place, we must admit that it would be unreasonable to suppose that no matter what kind

[1] St. John xiv. 2.

of a life we have lived here we should all automatically find ourselves in heaven when we die. Yet
that is a fairly popular presumption. It amounts
to saying that this life does not matter, and that a
man who cares nothing for God will nevertheless be
translated into his presence to serve him in the
eternal realm. There is nothing whatever in the
Christian Gospel to warrant such a belief. The
Gospel is presented to us for our acceptance, and
there is always in Scripture the utmost emphasis on
the eternal consequences of this choice. To reject
God's offer, to turn away from him, is a decision of
consequence. It is presented in the New Testament
as a literal matter of life and death. To be away
from God is hell. That is the definition of the word,
whatever picture-language may be used to speak of
its reality. The traditional Christian doctrine of
hell is actually one of the strongest affirmations of
man's free-will known to human thought. For it
contemplates the possibility of one of God's creatures
being able to say No to him indefinitely. When we
go on to ask whether the refusal of God can, in fact,
be eternal, or whether there must be a point when
either God's love must win every creature to himself
or else the impenitent must be finally destroyed, we
are in the realm of speculation where there is no
certain guide. All we know is that in the Scriptures
it is in the teaching of Jesus that most is said on this
subject; and his words suggest the magnitude of this
decision and the terrible consequences of a refusal.
While it would be true to say that the doctrine of an
eternal punishment of those who reject God, a
ceaseless torture such as has been described in the
more lurid portions of Christian preaching and
painting, is utterly inconsistent with the reality of

God's love for all his creatures, we must reckon with "the mystery of iniquity" and the stern words of Jesus about judgment.

We have, however, no grounds for limiting the participation in eternal life to those who have consciously received the Gospel of Jesus Christ. As we have noted before, many who have never heard of his name are nevertheless saved by the same grace of God which finds its perfect expression in him. That is to say that whoever is turned towards God in this life, wherever and whenever they may live, can share in his eternity. On all these questions true wisdom lies in a serious reckoning with our own position and a withholding of judgment upon others. God does not damn us: we damn ourselves. And we cannot assert of anyone else that they are bound for hell. To the multitude of questions that may be asked concerning the fate of hypothetical men and women, and concerning the possibilities in the life to come, we must steadily and soberly answer: I do not know.

The expression "the resurrection of the body" has raised difficulties for a great many Christians and enquirers about the Faith. It is connected in many minds with the notion that this body that we now possess is somehow put together again at a certain point in time. Such a notion involves so many impossible questions that it is hardly tenable for a moment's serious thought. Yet it has led to worries about the disposal of the dead, and anxieties about those whose bodies have been utterly dispersed in accident or warfare. It is natural for those who hear about a resurrection of the body to ask "With what body do they come?"[1] and yet it is to this very

[1] I Corinthians xv. 35.

question that the apostle gives the rough answer:
" Thou fool . . . God giveth it a body as it hath
pleased him." [1] The teaching is plainly that this
body that we know is *not* the one that we possess in
the eternal sphere. " It is sown a natural body;
it is raised a spiritual body." [2] What a " spiritual
body " can be we can have no idea, but the importance of the doctrine of the Resurrection is that it
means that our life beyond is a fully personal life,
dependent on the power of God to raise us up.
This is a quite different teaching from that of the
" immortality of the soul " which suggests that all
human beings possess an eternal something which
is released at death to form part of some greater
whole. The Christian Faith speaks always in
personal terms. The eternal life which it promises is
a re-creation of all that we mean by a " person "
here and now.

How is all that we have been considering about our
personal fate to be set in the wider picture of the
destiny of mankind? For we must remember that
the Christian Faith is not simply a method whereby
individuals are saved out of this world: it involves
a redemption of this world. And the coming
of Christ has significance for history, imparting
meaning, as we have seen, to the whole process in
time.

The dynamic conception of human destiny implied in Christianity has been given two very
different emphases.

(1) There are those whose eyes are resolutely
fixed on Christian achievement in the present world-
order. They take their inspiration from the words

---

[1] I Corinthians xv. 36 and 38.
[2] I Corinthians xv. 44.

of Jesus about the Kingdom of God growing like the mustard-seed, and the teaching of the apostles about service to humanity. With an optimism that is sometimes blind to the realities of human sin they set no limit to what can be achieved by the power of the Spirit of Christ within history. In the first flush of reaction to a barren orthodoxy which concentrated on the eternal world and consigned the present order to the devil, they proclaimed the transforming dynamic of contemporary Christianity.

> " Rise up, O men of God !
> His Kingdom tarries long;
> Bring in the day of brotherhood,
> And end the night of wrong."

The mood was impatient; the faith simple. With God's help men of goodwill could reach the Kingdom of God on earth.

(2) In our own day the wheel has turned again, and the current reaction against this optimism is as strong as its original impulse. Two world-wars, plus a return to the total witness of Scripture, have led Christians to revise their ideas of the extent to which the Kingdom of God can be realized in this era. Attention has again been turned to the eschatological element in the Gospel, and particularly on the Continent of Europe, where the experience of war was grimmest. Under stress it is natural for men to place their hopes for the future in a divine intervention rather than in a process of human evolution towards the Kingdom of God. Thus the elements in Scripture which refer to a return of Christ at " the end of the ages ", and the theology of a transcendent Kingdom belonging to a sphere beyond the present, have replaced in men's

minds the hopes of winning the world for Christ and
his Gospel.   The mood of the twelfth-century hymn
is in some ways nearer to us than that of the one just
quoted :

> " O come, O come Immanuel,
>   And ransom captive Israel,
> That mourn in lonely exile here
>   Until the Son of God appear."

Is it the Christian view that this world is a " lonely
exile ", or is it a place where men of God can rise
up and bring in the Kingdom?   Have we a hope
that the Spirit of Christ operating in the lives of men
can banish all evil, or are we to expect evil still to
flourish until Christ returns in triumph?   Is the
primary duty of the Christian to " let your light so
shine before men that they may see your good
works " [1] or is it to " watch and pray "? [2]   Is the
dynamic of the Christian message operative in
the redeeming work and service of the Church, or
is it a hidden power to be revealed at the end of
time?

That this cleavage of opinion goes deep within the
Christian Church today was evident at the World
Council of Churches Assembly at Evanston in 1954,
where the subject was " The Christian Hope ".
Yet it is plain that the cleavage is not complete, that
each way of thinking contains a permanent truth of
the Christian Gospel, and that each may be framed
in such a way as to obscure the real force of the
message.   In the light of Scripture and the experience of the Church some things can be stated
beyond all ambiguity.

(1) The destiny of man is in the hand of God, and

---

[1] St. Matthew v. 16.
[2] St. Matthew xxvi. 41.

not determined by any immanent law of progress. Belief in such inevitable progress has waned not only within Christianity but wherever the impact of recent war and the prospect of nuclear war have made their impression. Over against contemporary pessimism and loss of nerve the Christian Faith maintains a confidence in God's purposes. This means that history is never seen as out of control, and that the end of the world, whenever it may come, will not be simply the result of an accident, natural processes, or criminal lunacy, but within the design of God, the Father almighty.

(2) The return of Christ is an expression signifying the end of the present era. It is spoken of in the Bible and in hymns in terms drawn from a Hebrew way of thought known as "apocalyptic". We cannot simply take all such expressions and metaphors in a literal sense, yet we have no right to dismiss this mode of thought (so familiar to Jesus himself) as outmoded. Christians believe that, as this world had a beginning, so it will have an end. And at the end Christ will appear as the fulfilment, and therefore the Judge, of the whole process. There is obviously room for much difference of opinion as to the advance of the Kingdom of God on earth before the end. Here, in particular, nothing can be proved by the citing of isolated texts, or even isolated passages. The only such text that is conclusive (just because it is inconclusive) is: "Heaven and earth shall pass away, but my words shall not pass away. *But of that day and hour knoweth no man*, no, not the angels of heaven, but my Father only." [1]

(3) Such a belief means for the Christian not

[1] St. Matthew xxiv. 35, 36.

pious resignation but resolute action. A great number of the parables were spoken to this very situation. The bridegroom was coming: therefore the wise virgins took their lamps and went out to meet him, while the foolish slumbered and slept.[1] The master was returning: therefore the talents had to be used, and not hidden in the earth.[1] The Son of man is coming in his glory: therefore we have to feed, clothe, and tend the miserable for " inasmuch as ye have done it to the least of these my brethren, ye have done it unto me ".[1] Nothing could be farther from the New Testament teaching on the Christian life than the theory that because we believe in the return of Christ therefore there is no duty laid upon us now to do his will and mitigate the evils of the world. To give a concrete instance: a Christian may devote himself to the United Nations Association, not because he believes that a successful UNO would usher in the Kingdom of God, but because he believes that this is one of the ways in which he can act in response to that love which redeemed the world on Calvary and will claim it at the end of time. The second coming of Christ is a terminal point for Christian thinking about this world, and it is in the light of this climax that Christian service is carried through.

An illustration of the power of this eschatological hope could be taken from the life of a prisoner-of-war camp during World War II. British troops who had been captured during the Battle of France lived for some five years in the hope of a victorious liberation. But two attitudes could be taken towards that hope. Either they could say: a liberating army is going to arrive from outside;

[1] St. Matthew xxv.

therefore there is nothing for us to do but wait and pass the time away. Or else they could say: a liberating army is going to arrive from outside; therefore we shall prepare ourselves for it, and keep as fit in mind and body as we possibly can. When the "eschatological moment" did arrive and the camps were freed it was noticeable that it was those who had adopted the second attitude who were able to take real advantage of their liberation. In the New Testament the final Christian hope is described in such a way as to stimulate an active response to the needs of this world.

(4) This belief in another world in the light of which this one finds its meaning does not mean that for the Christian Faith the present world is of little value. It is true that it is considered as a world that "passeth away" and Christians are advised to conduct themselves in it as if they were a "colony of heaven" in an alien land. But it is still the world that God so loved as to give his only-begotten Son. The material conditions of this life, the physical universe in which we are set, are not disregarded in favour of a spiritual existence. Still less are they considered, as in some religions, as in themselves a manifestation of evil. "The earth is the Lord's and the fulness thereof"[1] according to the Old Testament, and "the heavens declare the glory of God and the firmament showeth his handiwork".[2] Jesus himself showed so little trace of asceticism that he was branded as a "gluttonous man and a wine-bibber".[3] His apostles recommended the churches which they founded to work in the world with thankfulness for all God's good gifts. In all this the Hebrew–Christian tradition contrasts strongly with

[1] Psalm xxiv. 1. [2] Psalm xix. 1. [3] St. Luke vii. 34.

the dualism of the Greeks, who tended to oppose the material to the spiritual and regarded the body as the prison of the soul. The Incarnation means that God himself has entered into the substance of this physical world and that he is personally involved in human history. Therefore the Christian Faith fully accepts this world as the instrument of the eternal and regards the course of history with the utmost seriousness.

These beliefs are a sufficient incentive for action without our waiting for a solution to the detailed problems of eschatology. The Christian attitude to the interminable speculations aroused by the questions of evil, pain, and human responsibility is illustrated in the story of Jesus and the blind man. "And as Jesus passed by, he saw a man which was blind from his birth. And his disciples asked him, saying, Master, who did sin, this man, or his parents, that he was born blind? Jesus answered, Neither hath this man sinned, nor his parents: but that the works of God should be made manifest in him . . ." [1] and went on to heal him. The entire system of Christian Faith is a mere structure of words unless it is understood as a summons to action. To see human destiny as a drama with a divine purpose is not to rob it of significance but to invest it with more. It is a commonplace of moral philosophy that happiness is not attained when we make it our goal, and a similar reasoning will show us that human betterment is not achieved when it is our sole concern. Therefore the Christian Faith, when it is most truly eschatological, is in the end most practical.

To put it in the shortest and simplest way: the Christian Faith is this: commitment to Christ, in

[1] St. John ix. 1-3.

ARABIC ASTRONOMY BANKING BEE-KEEPING BIOLOGY
NISATION CALCULUS CANASTA CARPENTRY CHEMISTRY
OMMERCIAL CORRESPONDENCE COMMERCIAL TRAVELLING TO
ING CRICKET DRAWING DRESSMAKING DUTCH DUTTON
ELECTRICITY IN THE HOUSE ELOCUTIONIST EMBROIDERY
ENGLISH RENASCENCE TO THE ROMANTIC REVIVAL ROMANTIC
EVERYDAY FRENCH TO EXPRESS YOURSELF FISHING TO FLY
E BOOK GARDENING GAS IN THE HOUSE GEOGRAPHY OF
ONARY GERMAN GRAMMAR GERMAN PHRASE BOOK GOLF
GOOD FARM ACCOUNTING GOOD FARM CROPS GOOD FARMING
T FARMING GOOD GRASSLAND GOOD AND HEALTHY ANIMALS
GOOD POULTRY KEEPING GOOD SHEEP FARMING GOOD SOIL
E HINDUSTANI HISTORY: ABRAHAM LINCOLN ALEXANDER THE
AU CONSTANTINE COOK CRANMER ERASMUS GLADSTONE AND
MILTON PERICLES PETER THE GREAT PUSHKIN RALEIGH RICHELIEU
ODROW ... EMENT
LIAN ETTER
ENGIN ···· AND HE WILL BE ANICS
ODERN ORING
HILOSO HYSICS
PLUMBI YET WISER *Proverbs 9.9* UBLIC
RECKO USSIAN
: ITS AND PURPOSE SOCCER SPANISH SPE AND
SWA SWEDISH TEACHING THINKING TRIG METRY
BRI H RAILWAYS FOR BOYS CAMPING FOR BOYS AND GIRLS
FOR GIRLS MODELMAKING FOR BOYS NEEDLEWORK FOR GIRLS
OYS AND GIRLS SAILING AND SMALL BOATS FOR BOYS AND GIRLS
ORK FOR BOYS ADVERTISING & PUBLICITY ALGEBRA AMATEUR
ING BIOLOGY BOOK-KEEPING BRICKWORK BRINGING UP
NTRY CHEMISTRY CHESS CHINESE COMMERCIAL ARITHMETIC
TRAVELLING TO COMPOSE MUSIC CONSTRUCTIONAL DETAILS
NG DUTCH DUTTON SPEEDWORDS ECONOMIC GEOGRAPHY
ST EMBROIDERY ENGLISH GRAMMAR LITERARY APPRECIATION
VAL ROMANTIC REVIVAL VICTORIAN AGE CONTEMPORARY
FISHING TO FLY FREELANCE WRITING FRENCH FRENCH
OUSE GEOGRAPHY OF LIVING THINGS GEOLOGY GEOMETRY
ASE BOOK GOLF GOOD CONTROL OF INSECT PESTS GOOD
FARM CROPS GOOD FARMING GOOD FARMING BY MACHINE
D GOOD AND HEALTHY ANIMALS GOOD MARKET GARDENING
GOOD SHEEP FARMING GOOD SOIL GOOD ENGLISH GREEK
ORY: ABRAHAM LINCOLN ALEXANDER THE GREAT BOLIVAR BOTHA
RANMER ERASMUS GLADSTONE AND LIBERALISM HENRY V JOAN OF
AT PUSHKIN RALEIGH RICHELIEU ROBESPIERRE THOMAS JEFFERSON
HOME NURSING HORSE MANAGEMENT HOUSEHOLD DOCTOR
URNALISM LATIN LAWN TENNIS LETTER WRITER MALAY
ONENTS WORKSHOP PRACTICE MECHANICS MECHANICAL
MORE GERMAN MOTHERCRAFT MOTORING MOTOR CYCLING
PHY PHYSICAL GEOGRAPHY PHYSICS PHYSIOLOGY PITMAN'S
ESE PSYCHOLOGY PUBLIC ADMINISTRATION PUBLIC SPEAKING

THE TEACH YOURSELF BOOKS
EDITED BY LEONARD CUTTS

THE CHRISTIAN FAITH

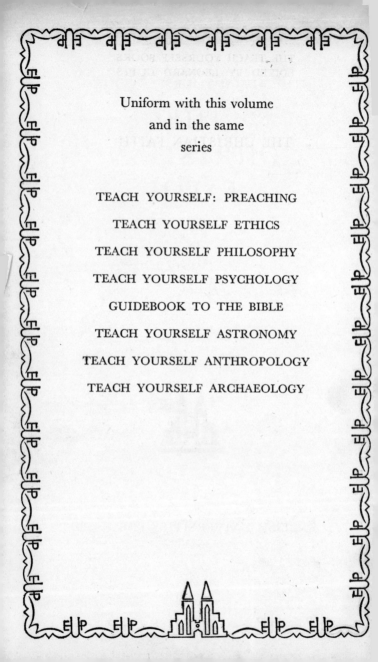

Uniform with this volume
and in the same
series

TEACH YOURSELF: PREACHING

TEACH YOURSELF ETHICS

TEACH YOURSELF PHILOSOPHY

TEACH YOURSELF PSYCHOLOGY

GUIDEBOOK TO THE BIBLE

TEACH YOURSELF ASTRONOMY

TEACH YOURSELF ANTHROPOLOGY

TEACH YOURSELF ARCHAEOLOGY

whom we find the love of God, and by whom we are enabled to love the Lord our God and our neighbour as ourselves.

For further reading:
  " And the Life Everlasting " : John Baillie.
  " Faith and History " : Reinhold Neibuhr.

ADVERTISING & PUBLICITY   ALGEBRA   AMATEUR ACTING   AN
BOOK-KEEPING   BRICKWORK   BRINGING UP CHILDREN   BUSIN
CHESS   CHINESE   COMMERCIAL ARITHMETIC   COMMERCIAL A
COMPOSE MUSIC   CONSTRUCTIONAL DETAILS   CONTRACT BRIDG
SPEEDWORDS   ECONOMIC GEOGRAPHY   ECONOMICS   ELEC
ENGLISH GRAMMAR   LITERARY APPRECIATION   ENGLISH RENA
REVIVAL   VICTORIAN AGE   CONTEMPORARY LITERATURE   ETC
FREELANCE WRITING   FRENCH   FRENCH DICTIONARY   FRENC
LIVING THINGS   GEOLOGY   GEOMETRY   GERMAN   GERMA
GOOD CONTROL OF INSECT PESTS   GOOD CONTROL OF PLANT DI
GOOD FARMING BY MACHINE   GOOD FARM WORKMANSHIP   GO
GOOD MARKET GARDENING   GOOD MILK FARMING   GOOD PIG
GOOD ENGLISH   GREEK   GREGG SHORTHAND   GUIDEBOOK TO
GREAT BOLIVAR BOTHA   CATHERINE THE GREAT   CHATHAM CL
LIBERALISM   HENRY V   JOAN OF ARC   JOHN WYCLIFFE   LENIN   LOU
ROBES...   HASTIN
HOUS...   ...EPAIR
WRIT...   ...ND TO
MECH...   ...LCRAF
MOTO...   ...FICIEN
PHYSI...   ...DESI
ADMI...   ...NG
PHR...   ...ACTIC
DEBAT...   ...DE

GIVE INSTRUCTION TO A WISE MAN...

...OOK   SAILING   SALESMANSHIP   SECRETA...
...SPELLING   STAMP COLLECTING   STUDE...
TYPEWRITING   USE OF GEOGRAPHY   WAY TO POETR...   W
COOKERY FOR GIRLS   DOGS AS PETS FOR BOYS AND GIRLS   KN
PHOTOGRAPHY FOR BOYS AND GIRLS   RADIO FOR BOYS   RIDIN
SOCCER FOR BOYS   STAMP COLLECTING FOR BOYS AND GIRLS   V
ACTING   ANATOMY   ARABIC   ASTRONOMY   BANKING
CHILDREN   BUSINESS ORGANISATION   CALCULUS   CANASTA
COMMERCIAL ART   COMMERCIAL CORRESPONDENCE   COMM
CONTRACT BRIDGE   COOKING   CRICKET   DRAWING   DR
ECONOMICS   ELECTRICITY   ELECTRICITY IN THE HOUSE   ELO
ENGLISH RENASCENCE   ENGLISH RENASCENCE TO THE ROMAN
LITERATURE   ETCHING   EVERYDAY FRENCH   TO EXPRESS YOU
DICTIONARY   FRENCH PHRASE BOOK   GARDENING   GAS IN
GERMAN   GERMAN DICTIONARY   GERMAN GRAMMAR   GERM
CONTROL OF PLANT DISEASES   GOOD FARM ACCOUNTING
GOOD FARM WORKMANSHIP   GOOD FRUIT FARMING   GOOD G
GOOD MILK FARMING   GOOD PIG KEEPING   GOOD POULTRY K
GREGG SHORTHAND   GUIDEBOOK TO THE BIBLE   HINDUSTANI
CATHERINE THE GREAT   CHATHAM CLEMENCEAU CONSTANTINE C
ARC   JOHN WYCLIFFE   LENIN   LOUIS XIV   MILTON   PERICLES   PETER
USE OF HISTORY   WARREN HASTINGS   WOODROW WILSON   HOC
HOUSEHOLD ELECTRICITY   HOUSE REPAIRS   ITALIAN   JOINER
MANAGEMENT   MATHEMATICS   HAND TOOLS   ENGINEERIN
DRAUGHTSMANSHIP   METEOROLOGY   MODELCRAFT   MODERN D
MUSIC   NORWEGIAN   PERSONAL EFFICIENCY   PHILOSOPHY   PH
SHORTHAND   PLANNING AND DESIGN   PLUMBING   POLISH   P